The **U**New **R** **B**Landsc**N**ape

The New U R

DRENTTEL DOYLE PARTNERS, *Design*

Olympia & York Companies (U.S.A.), *Sponsor*

B A N Landscape

R I C H A R D M A R T I N , *Editor*

TABLE

Olympia & York Arts & Events Program
Anita Contini,
Director
Melissa Coley,
Manager
Andrzej Drews,
Design Consultant

Exhibition/Education Committee
Gary Garrels
Barbara Jakobson
Peter Nagy
Lisa Phillips
Valerie Smith
Philip Yenawine

Exhibition and Catalogue Coordination
Livet Reichard
Company, Inc.
Ann Philbin,
Coordinator
Anne Blair Wrinkle,
Research

Board of Advisors
David Childs
Mildred Friedman

THE EXHIBITION: TWENTY

Frank Gehry
Richard Koshalek
Richard Martin
Cesar Pelli
Andrée Putman

This catalogue documents the exhibition The Nev

from October 14 through December 31, 1988, sponsored by Olympia & Yor

This exhibition was a part of the program to celebrate the opening of the the public spaces at Th

Printed in the United States of America.

Published 1990 by Olympia & York Companies (U.S.A.) and Drenttel Doyle Partners.

Library of Congress Catalogue Card Number: 89-063218
ISBN: 0-9624916-0-8
Distributed by Rizzoli International Publications, Inc.
300 Park Avenue South, New York, New York 10010

of # CONTENTS

Urban Landscape *held at The World Financial Center, Battery Park City, New York,*

Companies (U.S.A.).

World Financial Center.

Catalogue Concept, Design,
and Editorial Consultation

Drenttel Doyle Partners

Catalogue Editor

Richard Martin

Installation Design Concept

David Childs

Frank Gehry

Audrey Matlock

Artists and Architects, Vito Ac
Blum, Kim Adams, Judith Bar
Susan Hiller, Hodgetts + Fung
and Andrew Ginzel, Michael
Kunst Brothers, Justen Ladda,
Nouvel, Joel Otterson, Nam J
Price, Martha Schwartz, Haim
Ukeles, Jacques Vieille, Richar
Exhibition Video, MICA-TV;
Brooks, Bruce W. Ferguson, A
wick, Dave Hickey, Sanford Kw
Muschamp, Mark J. Plotkin, Na
Photographers, Jon Abbott, Davi

onci, Dennis Adams/Andrea
ry, Alan Belcher, Dan Graham,
Henry Jesionka, Kristin Jones
Kalil, Kawamata, Jon Kessler,
Morphosis, Matt Mullican, Jean
une Paik, Liz Phillips, Robert
Steinbach, Mierle Laderman
d Wentworth, Stephen Willats;
riters, Douglas Blau, Rosetta
dam Gopnik, Elizabeth Hard-
nter, Richard Martin, Herbert
ncy Princenthal, Mark Richard;
d McGlynn, Elizabeth Zeschin

THERE ARE MANY PEOPLE WHOSE HARD WORK WAS CRUCIAL TO THE SUCCESS OF THE NEW URBAN LANDSCAPE EXHIBITION. From the inception of the exhibition, the Board of Advisors, David Childs, Mildred Friedman, Frank Gehry, Richard Koshalek, Richard Martin, Cesar Pelli and Andrée Putman, lent their full support. The ideas and guidance from the Exhibition/Education Committee of Gary Garrels, Barbara Jakobson, Peter Nagy, Lisa Phillips, Valerie Smith and Philip Yenawine helped shape the show. Audrey Matlock of Skid-more, Owings & Merrill kept the exhibition design elements moving forward. 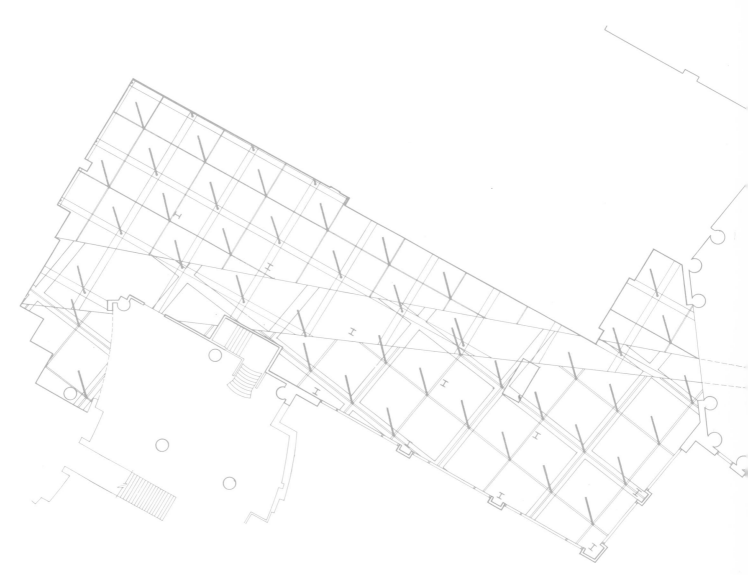 Anne Livet and Ann Philbin, the exhibition coordinator, as well as the staff of Livet Reichard Company, Inc., worked hard and long hours on the show—especially Nanna Kalinka Bjerke, Sylvia Escobar and Anne Blair Wrinkle. Crozier Fine Arts did a wonderful job installing the show—thanks to Peter Acheson, Bob Crozier, Robert Fosdick, Nathaniel Hupert, Bill Olson and Richard Sigmund. Also thanks to the staff at Drenttel Doyle Partners for their hard work on the brochure and catalogue. Irv Gotbaum of Brown

ACKNOW

8

& Wood was most supportive in sorting out all legal matters. The cooperation of Battery Park City Authority and the corporations at The World Financial Center deserves much appreciation, particularly that of Merrill Lynch, in whose building many of the works were installed. The Olympia & York Celebration Executive Committee of Anita Contini, Carol Friedland, Michael James, Philip Reichmann, Peter Rosenthal, Donna Smiley and Jerry Watson was most supportive throughout the entire process. The celebration staff of Robert O'Brien, Carol Ratnoff and Tracy Tooker kept everything moving. Special thanks to the construction and coordination groups at Olympia & York—John Caiazzo, Charlie Gazzola, Nick Giannak, Brian Gorman and John Norris—without whose help the show couldn't have happened. And very special thanks to Melissa Coley and Andrzej Drews whose dedication and hard work kept the installation process and the show itself running smoothly. Finally, and most importantly, thanks to the talented artists and writers without whose collective imagination and vision, this show and catalogue would not have been possible.

L E D G M E N T S

Plan for the exhibition
by **FRANK GEHRY**
in collaboration with **DAVID CHILDS**
and **AUDREY MATLOCK**
of Skidmore, Owings & Merrill

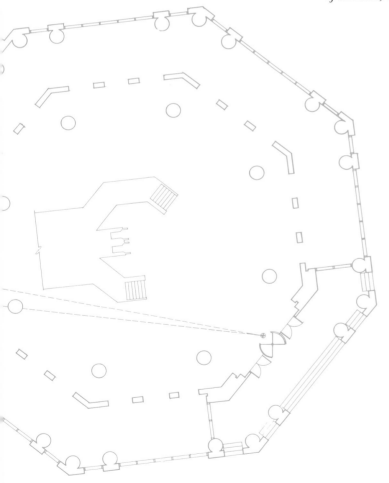

9

In October 1988, Olympia & York celebrated the completion of the public spaces at The World Financial Center. These grand public spaces comprise over 300,000 square feet of the 14-acre

INTRODUCTION

commercial complex located in New York's newest waterfront neighborhood, Battery Park City. A variety of free activities throughout these public areas was presented during the course of a five-day opening celebration. The Winter Garden, centerpiece of the indoor public spaces, was the site of perform-   ances by Cab Calloway and his Hi-De-Ho Orchestra, Kid Creole and the Coconuts, and the New York Pops. The Philadelphia Orchestra

with Isaac Stern and Mstislav Rostropovich performed at an opening night party to benefit "Stop Cancer." On the Plaza, the beautiful outdoor waterfront park, a 20-foot-tall warrior ant puppet was  part of a preview of a theatrical-musical work from the Brooklyn Academy of Music, along with live jazz and a dazzling display of fireworks. Other public spaces were animated with a Kid's

Fair, music from Bach to Broadway, and a commissioned dance work of brightly costumed mythical creatures by Alice Farley & Company. During this five-day celebration at The World Financial

Center, over 50,000 people of all ages visited and explored Manhattan's newest urban environment.

In addition to presenting events and entertainment, Olympia & York, as the developer of The World Financial Center, felt that the opening of the project's public spaces offered an opportunity to encourage community participation in a dialogue about the urban environment. In this spirit, The World Financial Center was the site of an exhibition, *The New Urban Landscape*, which started its three-month run during the celebration. Artists and architects were invited to create visual works that addressed issues about the "city," both positive and negative. And, as the exhibition addressed issues related to the urban environment, an opening-night party focused attention

on the global environment. This event benefited the World Wildlife Fund's Tropical Rainforest Conservation Program and was sponsored by Abitibi-Price. Performers included Grace Jones, Debbie Harry, Justin Hayward, Zoe Caldwell and the Saturday Night Live Band, who generously gave of their time to raise funds for this worthy cause.

This catalogue documents the art and architectural installations included in

The New Urban Landscape exhibition. In much the same manner as these works were commissioned for the exhibition, twelve writers were commissioned for

this catalogue to discuss our urban landscape. This catalogue brings together these artists and writers, who use imaginative and critical faculties, and often a sense of humor, to offer comments and schemes about urban life which affect us all. We appreciate their taking up this challenge in a public forum and engaging us in a thoughtful, timely dialogue.

ANITA CONTINI
Vice President & Artistic Director
Olympia & York

The city is an aesthetic expectation and plan, but the nature of that plan is also so idiosyncratically and socially determined that art and the city may seem irreconcilable, even while they are metaphors for one another. Richard Martin observes The New Urban Landscape: Spectators in the Visionary

IF, IN SPENGLER'S ADAGE, the narrative arts presuppose the world-city, the map and landscape of the city are the geography of the visual arts as well. The city that is microcosm of a world ⁓ even an uncharted sphere ⁓ and the macrocosm of art ⁓ even an inchoate aesthetic ⁓ is a metaphor as familiar as a city of God or an emerald city of longing and long dream. The artists of *The New Urban Landscape* enter into the persistent yearning of art indicative of complex urban life. Thus affiliated with art's abiding ambition and with urbanism's constant presence, these artists also reveal the particular character of the city today, an old idea in new forms.

Is the city today — or, at least, our perception of it — fundamentally different from the succession of cities that have previously existed? It may seem a vaunting zeal to pose a new city on the site of its multiple and continuous incarnations. Like modernism and modernity, the city is constantly reinvented in the mind and in its objects. Like modernism and modernity, the city in the 1980s poses the possibility of difference, or new inflection (which is not to argue for a factitious postmodernism that fades into nothing more than a newly inflected modernism), but a city that sustains the urban tradition, yet transfigures it in the specific habits of the 1980s.

Ever has the city been the site, for instance, of rapacious greed and the differentiation of classes determined in substance by money. There have been idyllic times when one sought the democratic city, whether in the idealism of public amenities and common grounds or in the expressed goals of shared values, but our decade has given little to unify the city. Instead, politicians build on their division of social classes, ethnic groups, and diverse interests to consolidate a stratum of power above adverse concerns and demands. Urban contrast is no longer a matter of crossing from one precinct into another, acknowledging that isolated problems exist, but the visible dialectic that universal problems permeate the opulent urban complex, made manifest in addicts that menace pedestrians wherever they walk, the shattered homeless who have taken the city at large to be what no designated site can be for their forced vagabondage, and the tolerance to such incivilities as trash and dirt that were once thought to be banished from the ivory colossus of the city. Under these circumstances, the traditional concept of grandeur for the city can barely exist. The urban metaphor in the 1980s requires new terms.

Roland Barthes tells us that de Maupassant, realizing that the Eiffel Tower was visible from every part of his city, determined to evade it by dining regularly in the restaurant there, enjoying not the food, but the opportunity to avoid seeing the monument. To be sure, in not seeing, he had become even more physically involved in the city's structure and in the very monument that he sought to elude. In the 1980s, art neither escapes the city nor does it perceive the city from on high. Rather, art addresses the infrastructure of human systems, technology, the environment, and the humane condition of the urban landscape.

Haim Steinbach's *Adirondack Tableau* may indicate the delicate place and the tough positioning of art of the city. Reversing de Maupassant's stratagem, Steinbach places his work on the bridge across Liberty Street (its name already redolent of urban history and dream) between windows into the urban direction and to the Hudson River. The traditional promise of art invested in nature the paradise of perfect forms only to be replicated by works of art in a naturalistic tradition or emulated by art of abstracting proclivity. Steinbach compels the contradiction and makes no reconciliation. He does not allow for art's easy triumph in tandem with nature, nor does he permit art to assume the autocratic and technological posture of a modern system capable of subduing nature. Rather, Steinbach's wall with aperture is more substantively a barrier than a passage. Discordant with the natural majesty of the Hudson, Steinbach's almost kitschy Adirondack environment is the perspective, from one side, of nature transformed into commodity and the self-consciousness of nature made into a convention. From another side, literally and figuratively, the ungrowing cabin-in-bench sward is anomalous with urban elevations beyond taking on the terms of advertising as if it were a billboard for holiday trips placed in an urban complex. What Steinbach has created is not convincing as a natural product, so manifest is its cliché of an urban phenomenon, so indefinite in the scale and decisiveness of urban expression.

It is, of course, an assertion about art, its title designating not only the vignette of wall and bench, but the French tradition of the grand painting. The wall, in this interpretation, is only a frame to the window as the traditional simile to the painting's eye and becomes insubstantial to the perspectives in two directions. Reduced to frame or focus, the wall becomes our point of perception for city and nature, both in their extreme forms, nature exemplified by the great river and the city by one of the tallest buildings in the world. Two hand-carved owls are the human simulation of a natural form, yet they are patently of the world of the humanly created, not of some taxidermy extending the real.

19

most radical gesture of the whole endeavor of *The New Urban Landscape* is that it has the site of The World Financial Center to speak the unmitigated truth of art.

The critical content of the art is not politely accommodated to its place. Instead, the confrontational clarity of purpose is evident in a number of works, including Dennis Adams and Andrea Blum's *Landfill: Bus Station,* an austere funerary monument that assumes a place in conjunction with the other art of the exhibition, but also imposes its strong sentiment on the daily life of the neighborhood as it fulfills its expressed function as a bus-stop bench. When bus shelters began to subsidize their specific function by attracting advertising, displaced from other common sites of the street, the excitement of the advertising, whether the allure of men's underwear goose-pimply provocative in winter weather or of romantic advertising for liquor offering a like seduction, became an expected device of contemporary urban life, adding to billboards, posters, and graffiti. That we are already inured to much of this advertising in the late 1980s is evident in the Adams-Blum transformation of the bus shelter into the more traditional tomb monument. Its structure altered and even less appealing or comfortable than most bus shelters, this bus stop is disquieting by its physical circumstances. The "advertising" that accompanies the structure explains the presence of death and gives death its specific indictment in South African apartheid. The dividing of the bench, its apparent hostility, and its discordance with comfortable urban amenity are an affront to the convention of urban relief, requiring nuisance, but insinuating the extreme form of annoyance that we call mortification. As a *memento mori,* the art succeeds because it involves the spectator/sitter in its bifurcation and its brutality; it challenges our notions of advertising; it calls to mind the history of objects and forms such as funerary monuments; and it is politically subversive with respect to one form of injustice (apartheid) yet abstract enough to suggest all malevolent mortification and death. In this respect, Adams and Blum have defied specific forms of contemporary life, yet have created a monument that transcends the particu-

We continue to need cities and we continue to need cities cognitively, needing to know how they work in order to help us understand how we work and how our world works.

These mystical observers possess, by tradition, wisdom. Steinbach's wise work of art is neither the triumph of nature or city; it is art's troubled truce between two powerful forces.

Given that one cannot avoid the city and its confrontations, the very place of *The New Urban Landscape* is an intrinsic part of its aesthetic and human message. Couched in the elegant luxury of Cesar Pelli buildings and assembled like squatters in the towers of corporate power that does nothing less than proclaim itself The World Financial Center, are art's initiatives annulled or, even worse, acquired by the prerogatives of real estate? Indeed, if the resolution of the works of art had been a platitudinous affirmation of the city, a glamorizing substantiation of urbanism (such as can still persist from 1930s dogma and earlier exposition), or a systematic beautification of the space in the naive tradition of highway beautification still espoused by Lady Bird Johnson, then the art would have ended up in service to other objectives. But what happened on Liberty Street is that aesthetic enterprise was as honored as any free enterprise. The comfortable circumstance of the art does not deny its discomforting and critical capacity. Rather, like the work of radical art seen in the modern museum, the strength of the art of social and cultural criticism is only exacerbated and enhanced by its placement in a position of some power. Art's voice, still dissonant and still dissenting, is more audible. Its language is not altered nor is its capacity to speak freely stifled. (On the contrary, art takes the rostra of commanding public discourse from the forum of public authority.) Perhaps the

lar place and the time to suggest a physical form for mourning, the defiant condition of scourging heaven, scorning humankind, and resigning life to earth.

Fundamental are the political convictions of artists in this exhibition. Tadashi Kawamata's *Favela in Battery Park City: Inside/Outside* likewise confronts The World Financial Center with what would seem to be its opposite. That this polemic occurs with sanction does not diminish the dialectic, but instead it permits and encourages our contemplation of the vast difference between the ad hoc and organic character of slum dwelling required for human existence and the opulent setting of The World Financial Center. To be the financial center of the world imposes a global responsibility evident in Kawamata's approximation of South American *favelas* or slum shanties and dwellings created with what may be described as an aesthetic lattice of available raw materials. The crudeness of the materials and the indiscriminate, almost chaotic, shape of the seemingly perilous construction assume their critical function in the work's simultaneous embrace and violation of the building, as the structure "grows" outside and inside. The principles of "proper" building are violated when the margins are broken and the ramshackle and indeterminate surpass the definite conventions of the building. Like a biotic excrescence confronting the structure of a modern — and especially refined — building, the Kawamata installation poses in aesthetic terms a substantive flouting of the conventional. In political and social terms, its improvised and needful forms generated by the way people build when their primary concern is survival, not the beautiful edifice, *Favela in Battery Park City* gives critical insight into the functions of a world financial network even beyond the particular city to a perception about the world.

The urban necessity of living and the concomitant determination of space is also the subject of Kim Adams' *Chameleon Unit.* Using truck sleepers, the yellow-green combination of the cornfield, and agricultural equipment, Adams seizes the mythos of the American Midwest and the open road to address the requirements of modern space. Adams' Midwest is far beyond Winesburg and beyond the bourgeoisie; it is the open terrain of the trucker, the stretched highway of cowboy-like independence and mores that has always blazed a trail in the American imagination. The trucker's sleeping quarters are the small elements of *Chameleon Unit*, its backyard placement (within The World Financial Center) evoking *Boy's Life* adventures even if limited to pup tents in the backyard. *Chameleon Unit* is a paean to independence and a reminder of the idealism of simple living in antithesis to urban life. But its placement in *The New Urban Landscape* alters its mobile meandering. When the range is supplanted by a street corner, the spectator peers with interest into its cabins, investigates the space, and may even reject the adventure. Demeaning as space independent of the mythos of the cowboy-trucker, *Chameleon Unit* sets up an urban *frisson* as unpleasant as recalling one's first search for an inexpensive studio apartment. In dialogue with the Kawamata structure on the north side of the street, Adams' sculpture seems mechanical and unromantic. Like Joe Buck in New York, the sculpture demonstrates the futility of a myth of the American West transposed to and encamped upon urban setting. While its elements come from the mobile sleepers, the addition of a screen and projection booth takes *Chameleon Unit* to the references of outdoor entertainments and fairgrounds as if this small unit were to be wheeled in to provide the fairground amusement of a brief moment. In this reference, there is the wistful world of tawdry small-town dreams difficult to reconcile with the Hudson beckoning scant yards away and elegant edifices of domestic and commercial life surrounding it.

Likewise, the rustic myth plumbed by Joel Otterson in *The Cage (The Living Room)* is the suite of discrepancies between our bucolic imaginations and the life of the city. More shocking than Courbet's rude peasants in the environs of sophisticated Paris, Otterson's chickens are a zoo's captive education expanded to the barnyard and the anomaly of rural commonplace to the "free-range chicken" gourmandise of contemporary urban life. Startling to find these hardscrabble fowl in the august place of art and commerce, *The Cage* poses the paradox of confinement, those in power and containment almost as fascinated by what is contained as their power on the outside. Otterson has made the cage structure a kind of *petit hameau* for urbanites, yet the artist is no Marie Antoinette as milkmaid. In fact raised on a farm, Otterson cultivates the paradox of Delft tiles on the ground and copper piping that reaches upward in cages that are simulations of modern office towers, yet were for the months of the installation the domicile of barnyard chickens. That urban visitors were often repelled by the odors and habits of these chickens was a bit like the provocation of bringing "noble savages" for exposition to London and the capitals of Europe.

There is an education even in repugnance. Had Otterson chosen rabbits or other more domesticated creatures for his crude/extravagant zoo, it would have been nothing more than an exoticism in art, but his determination to cull the barnyard is a tactic of confrontation and of resulting consequence for the urban visitor. A natural world does not end with flora; the animal life that Otterson brings to the city is a part of nature's continuity and the city's dependence. If the city is by metaphor a cage and urban life a rat race or other simile to the animal world, we see that metaphor to be true or false only in perceiving the cage. The untrammeled complacence of the chickens — albeit enjoying a quite tranquil and Perdue-free existence on prime Manhattan real estate — is, beyond odor or pecking and personal habits, troubling when one remembers that Otterson has equated in his title the cage and the living room. Veritably we all — whether urban or rural, high life form or medium — live in cages.

The fateful romance of the city and the country is realized in Justen Ladda's sculpture *Romeo and Juliet*, a late 20th-century bachelor machine in the Duchampian tradition, but with the added impact of cinematic convention as if a complex meteorite hurtling toward the small-town of cataclysmic adventure. If, in the imagination, the parklike star shape of the lower element is the unadulterated landscape with its ideal forms of trees and lakes (though Ladda has made this environment patently too meticulous, more in the manner of a golf course than raw nature), its reference vis-à-vis the urban mecanomorph above is the small town, the Grover's Corner that by infinite expansion is located in the eye of God. Bearing down upon it with Cyclops' eye is the technological form of the dynamo, the machine that is a compound of cities, countless houses, streets, and structures creating the equivalent of a child's "transformer," the 1980s toy that is both a human-referent and the multiplicity of mechanical interpretations. Dynamo and virgin land, this courtship as an above-

below coitus may seem as tragic, if as romantic, as Capulet and Montague. But Ladda has made of the machine/technology/transformer not a late 20th-century invention, but a city with colonial Revival buildings, churches, houses, a nostalgic city that is not advanced technology, but the evocative, historic, "livable" city of human proportions. In this decision, there is profound equivocation and Ladda's work is, on examination, not the foil one would imagine: city and country, dynamo and Virgin have seldom seemed so similar.

A related coupling occurs in Vito Acconci's *Garden with Fountain*, an exploration of space inside and out of the building, but also of the assumed dependence of two related forms. We make the assumption, wrongly in this instance, of the mutual affiliation of the garden and the fountain, as Acconci sets their relationship at the window of the building, frustrating any real interaction. The fountain plays its water with thwarted purpose on the window; bushes and trees grow on the inside without benefit of the continuous flow outside. Acconci has further made his garden as a kind of Rodia Towers of automobiles, but in *grisaille* akin to a clay model of the car design as much as to the car itself. He has returned the automobile to its nativity in a sense, making us see the car more generically and in genesis, rather than the specifics of an individual car. The rampant cars are piled up like an elegant multi-car wreck, yet never do they break the window. The comedy of *Garden with Fountain*, an antic work of art, is that this wreck seems to have occurred and yet there is no real breakage or source of the pileup, rather like the Chaplinesque comedy in which the protagonist causes everything to go wrong around him and blithely walks away from it all not realizing the havoc behind. At the line of the window there is a complete innocence of the deprivation and upheaval on both sides, an indifference that is a calm center in a work that juxtaposes urban accident and the placid potency of urban survival. Like twins and similar to Acconci's work in courting disaster, Richard Wentworth's *Neighbour, Neighbour* transforms the graspable house-shapes of the Monopoly game to giant caps suspended, with some trepidation on the part of the viewer, from the ceiling. If the most conventional views of family and domesticity are undergoing change, the enclosure of the house is capable of this transference from the benign to the invidious in a simple horror-movie transmogrification. What we have taken to be so appealing is now construed to be menacing. Like a poisonous apple pie or a child-abusing mom, Wentworth's house construction is the subversion of the accustomed and the tranquil.

The remarkable monument *Ruin* created by Nam June Paik is the accumulation of television sets (ascending to the present) as if they were the age-rings or stratification of modern media. That the movement across time now accompanies even the most casual observer's viewing of old television sets with a history barely exceeding the lifetime of adult viewers is an essay on recent history and its recollective, nostalgic impact. For those who might wish to recall the now-haunted world of "The Brady Bunch," yet claim as well the advances of VCRs and contemporary television, there is the opportunity to see both in one heaped-up form as offered by Paik. An artist long dedicated to an analytical understanding of television and video, Paik shows in *Ruin* a sad passage in time that can be read in several ways. A golden age of television may be recalled; television as a collective and family activity may be remembered; and video's individuation and personal selection may build upon, but constitute, the demise of broadcasting as a form of mass entertainment. Withal, Paik's use of relatively recent objects in their pyre suggests an Ozymandias of contemporary objects, an unceasing rejection of styles through design obsolescence and willed change, and finally our evocative memory of the objects now constituting a history.

The principles of "proper" building are violated when the margins are broken and the ramshackle and indeterminate surpass the definite conventions of the building.

How the city works, or, in some instances, does not work, is the exploration of many artists in *The New Urban Landscape*. That the modern urban condition employs symbolic language is evident in Matt Mullican's banner that harkens back to early identifications of feudal cities, but that also suggests the sign-system of contemporary life. Its popular or mass form evident in contemporary signage and graphic communication perceived as a scientific or social-science pursuit counterpoints its artistic form in the insistence on communications techniques appropriated from media, but fine-tuned in the fine arts. In this exercise, Mullican's art is symptomatic of its time in absorbing contemporary culture but insisting that art be the trenchant and transcendant medium to assess contemporary values. In so doing, the banner also signals some of the recurring preoccupations of *The New Urban Landscape*.

Mierle Laderman Ukeles created a like monument to the public infrastructure while preserving art's tradition and position of contemplation. Her *Ceremonial Arch Honoring Service Workers in the New Service Economy* is not only the elegant formal evolution of the arch in many constituent forms of urban workers, metaphors of hands, gloves, and running a gauntlet, but also the traditional form of art not alone in its structure, but in the

evaluation of contemporary culture. That Ukeles' insistence on new service professions stands only a few yards from Jon Kessler's elegy to the old industry in *Exodus* is a part of the dynamic of the artists in *The New Urban Landscape*. Kessler's essay in early 20th-century manufacturing employs the nostalgia of objects, but treats objects critically as well. Like Jannis Kounellis' Chicago evocations of the trains and sewing machines that symbolize industrial America, Kessler's machinery venerates a vintage America and reveals its mechanisms as if still clattering with power, yet even that noise and the office phone have become vehicles of forlorn repetition. The machinery of the garment industry that once was the major employer in New York City has exited in every way; it has gone offshore; the access industry for Jews in America has now enrolled other minorities; and its industrial triumph has been stilled by a post-industrial era in which manufacturing is newly conceived and realized. Together, these two essays in the history of the city move from production to service, from century's beginning to century's end.

In one form or another, the city has existed from the first communal impulses of humankind and from the kindred need for structures that serve both individual recognition and collective comprehension. We continue to need cities and we continue to need cities cognitively, needing to know how they work in order to help us understand how we work and how our world works. The world that John Winthrop wanted in America was called a city on a hill; the idea of perfection was termed a City of God; and the narrow interval between a human being and perfect attainment may always be called a city. Artists return again and again to the urban landscape to find the basest and the finest expressions of human configuration. City air sets free an art of beauty and inquiry.

23

The New Urban Landscape is a title that looks innocent enough but harbors vexing questions. Can a city maintain a memory of the land on which it is built❓ Does the image of a living, breathing natural environment provide a useful simile for the contemporary metropolis❓ And what can be called new about this peculiar organism❓ BY NANCY PRINCENTHAL

Robert Musil's description, first published in 1930, of "a kind of super-American city" ca. 1914 still serves. This city is a place "where everyone rushes about, or stands still, with a stop-watch in his hand. Air and earth form an anthill, veined by channels of traffic, rising storey upon storey. Overhead-trains, over-ground-trains, underground-trains, pneumatic Express Mails carrying consignments of human beings, chains of motor-vehicles all racing along horizontally, express lifts vertically pumping crowds from one traffic-level to another..."[1]

Musil's picture of mechanized, if exuberant, activity, and of atomization verging on dissolution, shows the urban sub-ject in a light that has bathed it throughout this century. In 1963, Lewis Mumford complained that "some of our younger architects and planners have been making sketches for an anti-city on the assumption that randomness, accident, defor-mation, fragmentation — like crime, violence, extermination — have the same order of value as function, purpose, integra-tion, health, moral character, or esthetic design."[2] He might have been talking about the work 20 years later of James

Wines, onetime sculptor, principal of the architectural firm SITE, and theoretician (who in fact shares more than a few of Mumford's views). "By insisting that a building stand for conditions of determinacy, structure, and order — a transla-tion of corporate America's values of investment, stability, and profits — twentieth-century architecture has consistently presented a false vision of the contemporary world,"[3] Wines writes. His proposed corrective is "de-architecture," which is a "way of dissecting, shattering, dissolving, inverting, and transforming certain fixed prejudices about building, in the interest of discovering revelations among the fragments."[4]

Together, these critiques suggest two parameters of the enormous territory covered by the installations in this exhibi-tion. But before they are addressed individually, some atten-tion should also be given to the term "installation." All 28 pieces on view were created just for this event — that is, they were commissioned. "Site specificity" is one notion generally implied by such commissions, and indeed the reason new work was called for was that the show's organizers wanted to give the artists an opportunity to address not just the nominal subject but also the context in which it was being considered. The context, in turn, involves not just the architecture of the exhibition space, but also the urban design, social engineering, corporate enterprise, and politics that impinge immediately and less directly on it, and on the relationship between sponsor and artist.

Finally, both subject ("the new urban landscape") and medium ("installation") imply a particularly intimate relation with the exhibition's audience; it is not wrong to say that much of this work is a kind of public art. The viewer and the viewer's experience of the site, the community, and the city, as resi-

THE NEW URBAN LANDSCAPE:

Public Art in Private Eyes

dent, employee, visitor, or observer, are what the work, in large part, is about.

Several artists and architects chose to address the metropolis as workplace, some considering it basically as an extensive physical plant. Mierle Laderman Ukeles, who has occupied the remarkable (and unsalaried) position of Artist in Residence at New York City's Sanitation Department for more than a decade, believes that "public art isn't something you just put in everyone's way — the *process* has to be public." And so her *Ceremonial Arch Honoring Service Workers in the New Service Economy*, initiated with the Sanitation Department's help, actively brought the department's employees together with other unsung maintenance people, including workers from the city departments of Cultural Affairs, Environmental Protection, Fire, Parks, Police, and Transportation; the state-run Metropolitan Transportation Authority; Con Edison and New York Telephone; the U.S. Postal Service; and Olympia & York; the Department of Sanitation in Tokyo even pitched in. Macadam, sod, mailbags, walkie-talkies, fire hoses, and the metal handles used by subway straphangers were among the donated "service-specific" materials used to form the columns supporting the arch, itself composed of the very visibly used workgloves sent by each one of the above agencies in response to Ukeles' request — in all, she received some 6,000 gloves. In one of the arch's two segments, these gloves are compressed within a metal armature; in the other, they reach out like the branches of a tree to form a more expansive and organic vault. Over all dance the red and blue lights of emergency vehicles.

Ukeles' sympathy for her subjects (she'd prefer "colleagues") is rare; quite literally, their work becomes her work, and in her ongoing representation of the city as a physical and social system she never conceals her respect for those who keep it running. Though Robert Price's view is both more abstract and, in a sense, more corrosive, he, too, rejects easy cynicism, intending his work to be seen as "friendly to the design of the building." *Face*, made of sections of brightly colored aluminum, is a large, rectangular column surrounding a forest of plumbing lines (the exhibition space was left fairly raw as designed by Frank Gehry, David Childs, and Audrey Matlock). An extravagant gold-tone bolt protrudes through each of the column's sides, and diagrams of various kinds of skin — human, geological, oceanic, atmospheric — are printed repeatedly over the column's "face." Around the bottom a frieze of maps of Manhattan is punched out of the aluminum, and other broad horizontal sections of the surfacing are left off on each side, revealing the installation's own metal struts and the building's substantial support lines, as well as miscellaneous construction debris. "It's like opening a vein," Price says, and the analogy is telling: where there is measured analysis in these installations, there is also not infrequently an undercurrent of violence, a destructive infrastructure.

Like *Face*, Alan Belcher's *Office Complex '88*, an elliptical gray structure partially sheathed in photographs of a building under construction, also treats issues of architectural and urban image-making. Formally and conceptually, Belcher's work turns in on itself like a clenched fist: its naked cinder-block walls and photographic exposure of structure are screens that only gradually reveal themselves to be impenetrable. In *Ecosystem*, an assemblage of traffic cones, sand, a potted tree, cobblestones, light reflectors, fencing, a tiny video monitor, and surveying equipment, Jean Nouvel creates a composite portrait of a typical city street, which since the advent of the automobile has been denounced (and occasionally acclaimed) by city planners for its dominion over the rest of the built environment. For a comprehensive view of the city as an architectural construct, there is Judith Barry's *Adam's Wish*, a video work projected onto an oval overhead screen that echoes the North Gatehouse's majestic rotunda above. Barry starts with the Sistine Ceiling, and accompanies the careening descent of modern man as he falls through a kaleidoscope of landmark structures, from the Pantheon in

Rome, to the Boston State House, to the Merrill Lynch Gatehouse. In the process, she reviews the architectural symbolism of authority, particularly as reflected in domes and rotundas, as it makes its transit from religious to secular language.

While these artists concentrated on the city's skin and bones, an equal number turned to industrial and corporate systems — the metropolitan body's sustaining fluids. Jon Kessler's *Exodus* is an imposing monument to the golden era of American manufacturing. A runway made of glass office doors, lit by incandescent bulbs flashing in sequence and traveled by a line of model airplanes, leads to a clattering mechanical dinosaur: an industrial knitting machine, turning out yards of gray wool suit material, some of which lines the runway. Attached to the machine's side is a faded photograph showing a prosperous-looking rust-belt plant, smokestacks blooming. As backdrop, Kessler preserved an un-sheetrocked section of the exhibition space's wall rich with building workers' graffiti. For a final touch, the runway is intersected by a metal office desk, on which sits an office phone, last year's model. Next to it, a speaker, endlessly repeating a recorded message: "the number you have reached . . . has been changed. The new number is . . ." Rust-belters take note; you can't go home again.

The tone of *Volta/Votive*, created by the Kunst Brothers (an art team consisting of Alison Saar and Tom Leeser), is also elegiac. A round structure modeled on nearby Castle Clinton, *Volta/Votive* is built of car batteries, a reference to the Battery of Battery Park and its new city, and also to the electrical juices that keep the city (local and general) going. Entry to the dark structure, carpeted with sand, is through a plus-shaped doorway, which frames a minus-shaped window on the opposite wall. At the center is a video monitor, face up and framed in brick like a primitive hearth; it shows images of fire, water, and a city in timeless flux. On the other hand, Stephen Willats focuses unflinchingly on the present. The realization of his *Signs and Messages from Corporate America* began with reconnaissance of office areas and building grounds in the World Financial Center complex. His concern is with the outer frequencies of what he calls "the bandwidth of the normal"; that is, he is interested in the expressions of personal will, sometimes overly oppositional, that can be found within the officially legislated visual environment. The objects of Willats' quest — a smiley label, an eraser stuck with pushpins, a photo ID card, a stuffed animal — were photographed, when possible with the owner/creator's willing engagement, and the resulting color images, custom shaped and framed, were matched with the corporations' own signatory artifacts: a logo, office equipment, building facades, official signage.

If the city is a corporate and financial stronghold, it is also, largely by consequence, a center of political power. Dennis Adams' and Andrea Blum's *Landfill: Bus Station*, a functional structure situated at a working bus stop, forces a captive audience to confront a haunting color photograph — placed where they might expect an advertisement — of several blacks carrying a coffin. As viewers may be able to surmise (though the photo's impact is potent even if they don't), the pallbearers are South African, and their burden is a victim of resistance to apartheid. The comfortless concrete bench from which one faces this document is shaped like an attenuated coffin, and, as the bench extends on both sides of the framed photo, violates it with calculated brutality. For would-be bus passengers, segregated by the barrier-like photo, waiting assumes the image of mourning (and sometimes even rage), or, perhaps, the resignation that can also be called complicity.

While Susan Hiller's *Monument* makes use of official (rather than subversive) commemoration of the dead, its subject is also working-class martyrs, and, more broadly, mechanisms of social control; in Hiller's words, the heroism at issue in her installation was fundamentally an ideological product. *Monument* is composed of color photographs reproducing a series of Edwardian English plaques honoring ordinary citizens, many of them young, who gave their lives to save others. "David Selves aged 12 off Woolrich supported his drowning playfellow and sank with him clasped in his arms September 12, 1886," one reads; "Soloman Galaman aged 11 died of injuries Sept 6, 1901 after saving his little brother from being run over in Commercial Street 'Mother I saved him but I could not save myself'" another. The 39 photographs are arranged in a cross formation, and in front of them is a bench like those from the park in which these plaques adorn a wall. On the bench is an audiotape on which Hiller discusses (among other things) the relationship between representation — which implies absence, and promises immortality — and death.

The city is not just a place where people work and govern, it is also a place where people — lots of them — live. Urban residence, and in particular the makeshift, free-form shelters contrived by Latin American urban poor, are Tadashi Kawamata's inspiration. His *Favela in Battery Park City: Inside/Outside* is a series of crude lean-to structures made from used lumber, its seemingly haphazard shape extending on both sides of a glass wall so that portions of both exhibition space and courtyard, including three trees, are consumed. Formed like a microbial growth, *Favela* suggests the susceptibility of a host body to organisms no less vigorous for their actual or social invisibility. But it also testifies to the transience of such victories, and the poverty of the conditions from which they spring.

Richard Wentworth takes aim at housing a few steps up the social ladder: his *Neighbour, Neighbour* consists of two Monopoly-style one-family houses made of rusted steel. They are bolted together with proudly visible hardware and suspended from the ceiling by a single cable, but between their adjoining walls is a thick layer of insulation, and connecting holes are plugged with cork. Hanging precariously on their tether, mercilessly exposed from below (they have no floors) but blind (they also lack windows and doors), locked in the uncongenial embrace of Siamese twins, these houses suggest the emptiness of conventional domesticity's ironclad comforts.

Sixty-five years ago Le Corbusier called the house "a

machine for living." It was in the trunk of a new car that modern technology arrived home, and the impression of the trip proved indelible. Like not a few designers before them, both Vito Acconci and Kim Adams have envisioned shelters as things built on wheels, modular and mobile. Adams' *Chameleon Unit* looks like a composite of doughnut truck, mobile home, and drive-in movie theater, but actually its three main units are salvaged "truck sleepers": bed-sized compartments, fitted with mattress and wheels, that attach to the big rigs. Two of these sleepers — in one, the bed has been replaced with a pair of tractor seats — are on an elevated platform that also boasts a large screen, wheel-mounted projection booth, and

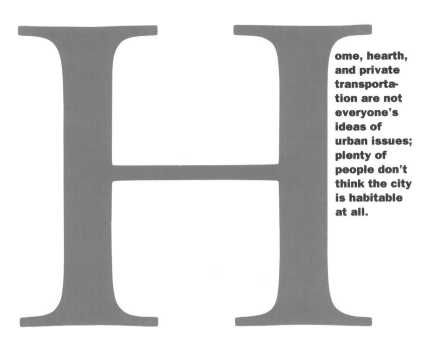

Home, hearth, and private transportation are not everyone's ideas of urban issues; plenty of people don't think the city is habitable at all.

viewing area with two lawn chairs. The third sleeper (the "master bedroom") is at street level. In its present context, the chameleon of the yellow and green structure's title is hopelessly (and quite humorously) prominent; in a cornfield, for instance, Adams says the unit, which is made in part from recycled agricultural equipment, would blend right in. Here, he adds, it looks "like toasters, or piggy banks." The associations are welcome; Adams (who was approached during installation by a shoeshine man envious of the artist's ability to gain sidewalk access and eager to go into partnership) is fascinated by the relationships among commerce, home building, and entertainment, and between all of these and art.

Though previously Acconci has also fitted cars with the accoutrements of home, his installation here renders the automobile wholly dysfunctional. Like Kawamata's *Favela*, Acconci's *Garden with Fountain* extends through the building's glass wall. A handful of cars, slathered heavily in tombstone-gray concrete, are piled up on either side of the window in what looks to be a crazy but serious monument to some con-

siderable wreck. From beneath the open hood of the uppermost outside car, a fountain sprinkles cheerfully against the glass. Bushes grow from the trunk of its indoor mate, and trees from its neighbors' hoods. As Acconci knows, we expect no less than water and greenery from our public amenities, however straitened their circumstances. And as is his wont, he obliges these expectations only to subvert them with imagery that speaks — in both formal and narrative terms — of violent collisions.

Home, hearth, and private transportation are not everyone's ideas of urban issues; plenty of people don't think the city is habitable at all. Just how far we have strayed from the natural environment is the question taken up by several artists who have examined urbanism in terms of its complement: the countryside and the life it supports. The approach taken by the architectural partnership of Hodgetts and Fung is something of a parody of objectivity. Their *Near Things* consists of five cinder block columns dedicated to grass, tar, refrigeration, ants, and water. These do not break down into neat nature/artifice categories, though the columns look cleanly scientific, each suggesting a vertical sample of some hypothetical community's physical basis. On examination, the parts are joyously strange: a child's wading pool bathes the foot of one column, which supports a rectangular wired-glass tub of aqua-tinted water; the air from two blow dryers gently ruffles the grass on another. Most mesmerizing, and most easily likened to the metropolitan experience, are the ant farms, visible in Plexiglas boxes and also enlarged, on a video monitor.

Long interested in the relation of suburb to city and of public to private space, Dan Graham has constructed a small pavilion that refers to both garden gazebos (in form) and high-rise office towers (in materials). *Triangular Structure With Two-Way Mirror Sliding Door* is a discreet structure made of two-way reflecting glass, a favorite material for Graham. Tucked into an exterior corner of Two World Financial Center, it accommodates only a single viewer comfortably. The mirrored walls superimpose that viewer's reflection on direct and reflected vistas of the courtyard and riverscape beyond. Permeability is multiply confused — the walls are both opaque and transparent, the floor is a metal grid of the kind used for subway grating, and the ceiling is glass — just as the limits of illusory and real presence are confounded. Moreover, the country and the city are made to mingle, as sky, water, and buildings near and distant take their places on the reflective surface.

Nature and culture are nowhere more graphically opposed than in Justen Ladda's *Romeo and Juliet*. Hovering just above a star-shaped model of sylvan meadows, woods, and river is a predatory form that takes its basic shape from an automobile engine. A gear shift protrudes from its front end, and a detailed depiction of the engine is painted in grisaille on one side, rendered in Ladda's trademark one-point perspective so that it is clearly legible only from a certain place on the floor. The engine is composed entirely of miniature models of city buildings, which are painted in naturalistic colors on the other side, and on all but the leading faces of the first side as well. The installation's title helps tell the story: an irresistible attraction draws country and city together, with consequences ultimately fatal for both.

Of course, the dream of return to a natural paradise is irrepressible. Haim Steinbach's *Adirondack Tableau* illustrates its commodification. Two rustic, Adirondack-style benches flank a rough, cedar-shingled wall, in the window of which sit two wooden owls, intricately handcrafted by a professional artisan. Steinbach's installation is in an overhead walkway connecting two buildings, and the benches offer views of the Hudson and the financial district, but the implicit choice between natural and man-made is deceptive. No less than the canyons of Wall Street, the "natural" environment available to the average urbanite is a product of sometimes artful, sometimes irresponsible human enterprise. Joel Otterson's *The Cage (The Living Room)* observes nature not so much commodified as domesticated. As funny as it is deceptively simple, Otterson's idea was to present caged animals — the analogy to city-dwellers is venerable — but with a double twist: the wheel-mounted cages are decidedly luxury models (they are paved in authentic Delft tiles, lit by rococo porcelain chandeliers, and framed in copper piping and wire mesh that rise in twin skyscraper configurations to blue-glass ceilings), and the residents are unmistakably low-rent animals (half a dozen white barnyard chickens). Otterson, who was raised on a farm by a father who doubled as a plumber, says the piece is autobiographical, though it was precipitated by a visit to a 19th-century zoo in Antwerp where the animals are housed in Egyptian temples, Swiss chalets, and other all-time architectural favorites.

While Steinbach and Otterson oppose vernacular images of rural life to the contemporary urban experience, others go beyond the inhabited countryside to consider the landscape itself. Jacques Vieille and the architectural team Morphosis both use caged trees to suggest the present deracination of even the most elementary components of our natural environment. In Vieille's *14 Arborvitae,* each of 14 potted evergreens nests inside a fan-shaped wooden armature loosely evocative of some large tropical bush. Placed inside The World Financial Center lobby in an arrangement carefully calibrated to respond to its architectural context, these repeatedly displaced trees are both supported and inhibited by their wooden cages. Morphosis' *Room Compressed,* situated outdoors in the circular driveway, traps a single evergreen, its roots wrapped in burlap, within a wood and metal framework, itself clamped between steel plates and winched to substantial metal bulkheads. Despite the evidence of effort out of proportion to the task, the tree remains just outside a central depression in the stone-paved traffic island it dominates, an icon to comically misspent energies and, possibly, the ultimate intransigence of nature.

Landscape architect Martha Schwartz considers the

contest to have been long won by the cages and clamps. Rather than introducing natural vegetation to built form, she therefore creates parks and gardens entirely of artificial materials.

In *Turf Parterre Garden* she has used rectangles of Astroturf, her medium of choice, and cut them to the size and shape of the windows on the North Gatehouse's facade. These sheets of Astroturf are adhered to the side of the building, starting three stories below the top, in a grid that duplicates the fenestration but is slightly skewed. Where the Astroturf pattern hits the ground, Schwartz continues it by removing window-shaped squares of sod from the existing lawn. In its integration of building and context, *Turf Parterre Garden* maintains a healthy skepticism about the "nature" of the building's "ground" — both these terms come under withering scrutiny in Schwartz's work — while also preserving faith in the tower's formal integrity. For the many artists to whom the city means neither workplace nor residence, nor nature trammeled or triumphant, the urban landscape is above all a spectacle of technology's sometimes dubious progress. Nam June Paik, éminence grise of video art, has created for this exhibition a pile of 45 "antique" (that is, 30-year-old) TV cabinets dotted with 24 new video monitors, each playing a quick-dissolving, much fragmented montage of urban imagery. Paik's *Ruin* is a contemporary relic on which new media life has sprung up like weeds on the Acropolis. Henry Jesionka's *Nullstadt,* for "no city" (or none with a fixed identity), takes an even more nostalgic approach to modern technology, applying the principle of the camera obscura, popularized in the Renaissance, to the representation of riverfront activity at Battery Park City. Ten lenses, some filled with water (to both optical and associative effect), focus pinpoints of daylight into an unlit room, providing romantically diffuse reflections of passersby outside. These images, in which scale and position are subtly distorted, cascade over walls and ceiling, while a mechanical seismometer senses movement of spectators inside the room, projecting these in the form of a fluctuating red laser beam. Jesionka's belief that the city is best understood as a temporal rather than spatial experience, where no perspective is stable and no view exhaustive, is clearly expressed in this installation. The collaborating sculptors Kristin Jones and Andrew Ginzel have also produced an image of technology steeped in reverie. Their *Geotaxis* is a glass-fronted diorama set in a space that could serve as a retail display window. Its shifting sands, revolving hourglass, gold-leafed, three-bladed propeller, spinning balls, and painted poles, all set against a metallic-striped background, together evoke mechanical invention in the golden age of alchemy, when science stole scholastic ground (and credence) from religion.

Other artists — they are few — stare resolutely into technology's future. Michael Kalil is a designer for NASA and an occasional sculptor of installations that create the illusion of weightlessness. His *Elysian Field III A* consists of a large crater, above which two spheres hover without evident support. Painted white, sheltered by a segmented wall, and bathed in a pale violet glow, these forms suggest 20th-century physics' successive disembodiments of matter. More specifically, *Elysian Field III A* relates to a living room Kalil is now designing for a future generation of space stations. In Kalil's conception, the urban environment has been divided into three: its "center" has no fixed place on the planet, but is any nexus of information from one or all of the three telecommunications satellites that link its population; the function of "neighborhood" now exists in the form of nationhood, or of geographically dispersed national identity; and the "edge" has been projected into outer space. It is for this edge that his several Elysian Fields are designed. Even without benefit of Kalil's explanation, his installation speaks of an independ-

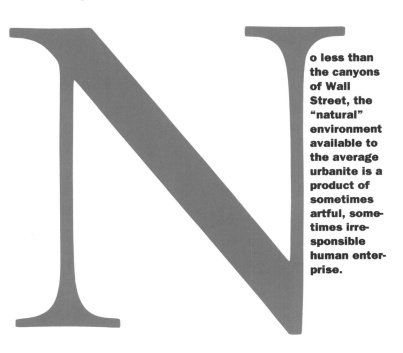

No less than the canyons of Wall Street, the "natural" environment available to the average urbanite is a product of sometimes artful, sometimes irresponsible human enterprise.

ence of gravity, a loss of social fixedness, that has long been popularly linked to metropolitan life. It is precisely the usually heedless trajectories of pedestrians across space that sound artist Liz Phillips takes as her subject. *Cymbal* is an interactive sound environment in which the path taken by each person approaching the exhibition's entrance is tracked by six ultrasonic sensors, translated into sound, and broadcast over three speakers in the form of electronically synthesized pings, chimes, growls, and clinks. This subtle orchestration of chance encounters and common purpose is, appropriately, neither harmonious nor dissonant. And while clearly audible (and visible — all the equipment is plainly shown behind clear Plexiglas screens), *Cymbal* hews to urban social conventions by engaging only the voluntarily attentive: it is easy to miss, or to consign to one's aural periphery. Equally apt for the New York audience, it especially rewards the listener in motion, though the temptation to linger is strong.

What Phillips has done for the exhibition-goer, Carole Ann Klonarides and Michael Owen of MICA-TV have done for the show's participants, allowing ten of the artists to articulate details about their presences that would otherwise remain tacit. In interviews and fast-paced image collages, this compilation of two-minute video pieces captures the hectic, wildly stimulating spirit of working at this scale in this context.

Haven for outspoken (and even conventional) idiosyncracy as well as for close-guarded privacy, the contemporary city answers to no single common language, though the totality of those spoken comprise its distinctive text. Matt Mullican's banner is a quartet of symbols that look universal but are in essence personal. The four symbols are a circle within a square (the sign of the sign), a circle within a human profile (the sign of subjectivity), a schematic globe, and four small circles signifying the elements. The positions of these symbols and the relationships between them ramify widely: the profile gazing at the sign that head the banner indicates, in Mullican's scheme, the dominance of subjectivity over the world and the elements as we know them; recognizable representation (profile and globe) balance and shape the meaning of abstract symbols. Further, yellow is, for Mullican, the color of the "world framed," or experience circumscribed by art.

Big and prominently positioned, the banner is both an individually expressive element of the exhibition and was appropriated as an announcement for it, even in promotional literature. Though he anticipated this duality, Mullican is ambivalent about the banner design's use for publicity purposes; he would like to collect the advertising material in which the piece is reproduced and fashion a new work out of it, tightening by a notch the orbit in which commerce and culture both spin.

The question of Mullican's role — herald or subject? reader or author? — can be generalized to his artist/architect colleagues, whose parts in shaping the contemporary city are at once responsive, interpretive, and transformative. It is a question that belongs with those fundamental to the exhibition, for certainly the new urban landscape would be unrecognizable without the kinds of effort made by the sculptors, designers, builders, and many other artists represented here whose work, after all these years of sloganeering, still defies categorization. In all its diversity, this exhibition emphasizes throughout that the city and those who define its visible (and otherwise perceptible) image live in an inextricably reciprocal relationship.

FOOTNOTES

[1] Robert Musil, *The Man Without Qualities*, New York: Perigee Books, 1980, p. 30.

[2] Lewis Mumford, "Beginnings of Urban Integration," *Architectural Record*, January 1963. Reprinted in Mumford, *The Urban Prospect*, New York: Harcourt, Brace & World, 1968, p. 143.

[3] James Wines, *De-Architecture*, New York: Rizzoli International Publications, 1987, p. 125.

[4] Ibid., p. 133.

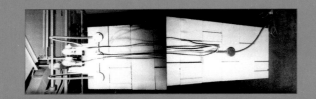

DAVID McGLYNN A PHOTO

30

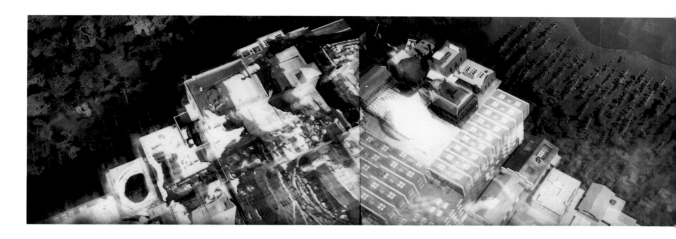

G R A P H I C ESSAY

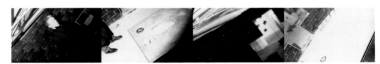

33

CITY TAKES

Ten Essays by **Douglas Blau, Rosetta Brooks, Bruce W. Ferguson, Adam Gopnik, Elizabeth Hardwick, Dave Hickey, Sanford Kwinter, Herbert Muschamp, Mark J. Plotkin,** *and* **Mark Richard**

The first request Gulliver made after obtaining his liberty from the Lilliputians

was for permission to visit the capital of their empire, the metropolis Mildendo, which lay a short distance – relatively speaking – from the beach where he had been tied. The sight of the city's towers in the not-too-distant distance, the puffs of smoke rising from ten thousand miniature chimneys aroused his curiosity. And, with passport in hand, Gulliver covered the distance between port and town in a couple of careful strides. ⌖ Sitting on a hillside overlooking Mildendo's walls, Man-Mountain surveys the scene: a model city whose architectural details are familiar in every respect, with the exception of their Lilliputian size. No doubt the view makes this onlooker feel as if he were somewhat out of sync mind – for how will he fill his belly in a flower bed and cattle stand four and a

Brobdingnag

and, no doubt, certain fears cloud his world where a farm is no bigger than a half inches high? But concerns over dis-location fade as he considers the advantages that his unique vantage provides: nearly two centuries before man learns to fly, Gulliver sees an entire city from the sky. In an instant, he grasps the logic of its overall design. ⌖ BY DOUGLAS BLAU

37

Streetwise

ROSETTA BROOKS

DOWNTOWN Manhattan: A bag lady and a security guard eye each other suspiciously across the polished concourse of a shopping precinct. There's a battle going on here for spatial domination between opponents who recognize each other easily by their respective uniforms. For other shoppers in the mall, the woman's partially exposed feet in their ill-fitting trainers signal clearly that she is trespassing. And, while the security guard's job is mostly to move on such unwanted people, he rarely has to do so. His appearance is usually enough to discourage loiterers.

In the end, the bag lady will have to move on, for there's no such thing as civic rights in these privatized streets. A homeless woman with her entire possessions in dirty brown bags is an unwelcome intrusion in these synthetic spaces created as barricades against the harsh realities of the streets to which she has been condemned.

Uptown, the Bronx: Eye contact between the two men is issued as a challenge; throwing down the gauntlet between drug dealer and junkie. The noise of the bullet fired from a .357 magnum that tears the young man's head open is just another sound of the city. But the body lying on the sidewalk is not so easily camouflaged; it remains there for more than five hours. Passersby accept the violence casually. "Some dude didn't pay his debts," remarks one 11-year-old to his friend.

These kids know more about the streets than you would ever want to know.

LEWIS MUMFORD describes the city as "the point of maximum concentration for the power and culture of a community," a place where "the diffused rays of many separate beams of life fall into focus," and where we witness "the form and symbol of integrated social relationships." He saw the city as a work of art, a collective dream that nurtures the desires and dreams of its inhabitants. It's not that Mumford got it wrong. It's just that the definitions of "community" and "collective dream" are not the same anymore. Mumford's ideas were predicated on the utopian belief in a democratic view of urban renewal and in a commonly held confidence in civic consciousness, both of which are as foreign to the contemporary city as was social mobility to the medieval city.

For what kind of dreams lie beneath the spatial schizophrenia of our contemporary cities? What visions are nurtured in the gaps between the vacated opulence of the shopping precinct and the crowded dereliction of the streets? In the 1980s the clean and dirty, the order and chaos, the heaven and hell of the city exist side by side.

NOT SO LONG AGO, urban space seemed to offer a different picture: A threat of anonymity, uniformity; where the sense of a local community was being replaced with concerns for universality; where blandness and sameness were becoming the order of the day, ousting difference and originality. During those early postwar years, it looked like the fate of the modern city was fast becoming a triumph of order over chaos. A city of entropic spaces.

But that's all changed now. The past two decades have revealed a conspicuous countertendency. Our cities have become fractured, disassociative, spatial environments where boundaries have become exaggerated and almost tangible.

38

City space encourages a heightened state of anxious vigilance now, and walking the streets compels you to pay close attention to every configuration whose slightest shift can insinuate foreboding or anxious checking, or intimidation.

STREETS ARE no longer crowded, reassuring seas of anonymity in which to feel either alienated or at home. Entropic spatial anonymity has given way to a more powerful spatial estrangement, threatening and dangerous to the max. Street life in the modern city has become the darkness and chaos — both imaginary and real — of malevolent forces from which the medieval city fortified its inhabitants. With the demise of the Welfare State and the closure of mental institutions, the streets are full of the dispossessed, the abandoned and the homeless once again. Street life today represents a new kind of spectacle. From the neurologically dysfunctional and homeless ex-inmates of mental wards, through the bums begging for a quarter who frequently have a better rap than most television comedians, down to the crack addict whose pleasant disposition can as easily turn to soured aggression, street culture is now made up of overdoses of fear, addiction and violence. In this macabre dance of death, streets have become the vortex of a downward spiral portraying an imminent threat of dispossession through their chaotic images and pattern.

CONVERSELY, middle-class districts in the modern city have reproduced exactly the conditions of the medieval fortifications that would later become known as cities. Today's cities, to a large extent, have returned to their origins. High-rise buildings and apartment complexes in these neighborhoods are like stockades protected by high walls, patrolled by private police and screened by all kinds of surveillance apparatus and security agencies. Cities within cities.

FOR TRADITIONAL theorists like Mumford, the modern city is characterized by speed. The instantaneity of electronic technologies has turned cities into national and international headquarters for financial, political and industrial enterprises whose primary technological hardware consists of Fax machines, Express Mail and other telenegotiation systems, an array of satellite scanning devices that move information across the planet at the flick of a switch. Yet by contrast, the experience of the city for its residents is a network of stoppages, punctuated and interrupted by security thresholds. Delays are created, for example, by the simple act of unlocking steel doors to cross the threshold from street to apartment; self-consciousness is felt whenever we enter buildings with the presence of surveillance cameras; self-scrutiny is involved every time a stranger approaches us on the street as we choose automatically from a variety of social masks to neutralize feelings of apprehension. Our cities are now both psychological and physical intersections. They are spaces of surveillance and orders of control. Primitive instincts have become absolute necessities.

WE EXPERIENCE urban space as fragmentary, discombobulating and shaped by a complex sign system of inclusion and exclusion. In a more threatening sense than in the medieval city, streets are now, first and foremost, lines of communication whose correct reading can be a matter of life and death. City streets act as constant reminders of the precarious precipice that — in a moment of violence or in a sudden change of fortune — can reverse the roles of winner and loser. Hiding behind the appropriate mask, using our instincts, getting the signs down: These are the nuances we cultivate for survival in the metropolis. And they are all as critical to survival for the bag lady as they are for the stranger asking directions in an unfamiliar area.

BRUCE W. FERGUSON

Word
Trade
Center

The city, like the computer, is an influencing machine. Like the programs and applications embedded at a *sub rosa* strata within the computer, the city is also deeply configured as an inflationary language bank. By driving the logic tree (eliminating specific tautologies and redundancies) of the thesaurus function, it is possible to uncover the hidden narrative (agenda) at the intersections of their limits. The following are the first 500 words (generated by the first 58) to be discovered in a search toward a (maximum) representation of power.

city: borough: megalopolis: metropolis: municipality: district jurisdiction precinct ward suburb: town: burgh: community settlement community: citizens crowd culture folks group (human) beings individuals laity masses men (and) women neighbors people persons populace population public society staff brotherhood camaraderie *esprit-de-corps* fellowship fraternity lodge settlement: arrangement franchise municipality: district: area domain environs locality neighborhood province range region section sphere vicinity zone jurisdiction: authority command commission control direction domination management mastery might power rule precinct: ward: alcove chamber room citizens: crowd: assembly caucus conference congregation convention council gathering meeting rally symposium band bunch crew gang huddle mass mob pack rabble riffraff swarm team throng compact compress crush jam mash pack press culture: education development folks: group: association band bevy bunch camp clique cluster collection organization party cartel coalition collaboration combine conglomerate consortium federation pool syndicate trust breed category division genre genus ilk lot section sector set sort species type concentration lump mass rally rendezvous alignment assortment pigeonhole place position program rank rate sort stack human being: homosapiens individual man person woman mortal entity object organism system totality whole actuality existence fact life presence animal monster ogre individuals: laity: devotees fold followers members parishioners masses: men: army battalion brigade company force gang power soldiers troops (and) women: **THE WORD WAS NOT FOUND. CHOOSE ANOTHER WORD TO LOOK UP.** neighbors: people: family kin relation relative employees faculty help personnel staff workers breed clan class household race relatives stock persons: populace: population: public: collective common social societal visible settlement: society: institution organization union body club company delegation fellowship fraternity guild brotherhood: *camaraderie esprit-de-corps* outfit troop troupe fellowship: corporation establishment foundation fraternity: companionship friendship intimacy lodge: abode bungalow co-op hutch hovel shack shanty hotel inn dwelling nest quarters station franchise: charter hire lease let permit rent sublet area:

A journey from city to theory in 500 words of frustration, exchange, transaction

locus place point property scene site spot land patch sod space turf arena belt field realm region section territory tract domain: dominion kingdom sphere territory acreage estate grounds holdings land real estate environs: jurisdiction: locality: neighborhood: province: range: spread compass confines dimension distance extension length limit orbit purview reach scope size spectrum sweep width breadth depth dimension span boundary vicinity region: section: passage portion division lot member parcel part piece segment slice addition annex branch extension wing sphere: vicinity: nearness proximity zone: location authority: clout control influence power prestige pull brass elders leaders officers command: influence commission: administration administrators authorities bureaucracy department forces government ministry officials powers rulers ante award bonus booty cash dividend donation fee gift gratuity largess money percentage perk prerequisite premium prize profit purse reward sharing stake stipend tip winnings bill bonus charge compensation consideration earnings fee gross income pay revenue salary wage warrant board cabinet committee council directorship accredit authorize certify empower enable entitle facilitate invest license permit sanction validate charter engage direction: directive guideline instruction outline policy domination: management: charge conduct handling intendance overseeing running supervision mastery: might: ardor beef brawn drive energy force intensity lustiness muscle pep potency power punch steam strength verve vigor vim virility vitality rule: announcement aphorism axiom cliché declaration decree dictum belief canon code conviction creed doctrine dogma law opinion principle tenet theory ✒

I don't think that I understood the relationship between the generic and the particular in New York until this past Sunday.

That was when Dean & Deluca, the Soho grocery store that has been on Prince Street between Greene and Wooster for the past decade, closed its doors; the owners are opening a new, much bigger place on lower Broadway. My wife and I have lived in a small loft in Soho for the past five years — half of Dean & Deluca's life — and on Sunday afternoon we went to peer into the windows of the new space on Broadway. It was immense, four or five times the size of the old place. We saw big, empty refrigerator cases, right up front, meant for fresh fish and meat (at the old store they never had the inclination, or the room, to sell those things). There was an espresso bar with a marble top — they never had *that* at the old place either. And rows upon rows of expectant, empty steel shelving. We went back to the old store, bought half a pound of Black Forest ham (for only a little bit more than it would cost you uptown at Schaller & Weber) and watched the Prince Street store close. We felt surprisingly sad, considering that what we were losing was only a store, after all. We're not so D & D dependent that a few days without the chance to buy imported goods at inflated prices is going to leave us emotionally distraught. And if Dean & Deluca was in some ways clubbish, it wasn't a

club that we really belonged to. Certainly not the way some painters did. I once watched one of the doyennes of the new image painting finish up an order on a fall afternoon; she picked out vegetables as perfectly as she painted clouds. Just watching her check out was something. Clerks came over from the cheese department to look.

But every generation, arriving in New York, discovers a few places that seem to belong to it, and Dean & Deluca was for my wife and me what the Museum of Modern Art garden was to my parents, or what the Roxy and the Paramount were to my grandparents. When my wife and I arrived in the city, in the late seventies — me hoping to study pictures, my wife hoping to paint them — we would get on the subway and go down to Soho every Saturday morning. On the subway headed downtown, on the streets of Soho when we arrived, there would be what seemed thousands of couples who looked and dressed and gazed at things exactly the way that we did. And the path we would all follow for the next few hours, though it was, of course, never discussed, much less written down, was as universally adhered to as any pilgrimage path. You would begin at Four Twenty West Broadway — walking all the way up to the top, and then working your way, floor by floor, gallery by gallery, downstairs. When I am eighty, I am sure that I will lie in bed at night and remember the descending order of galleries: Charles Cowles, the Forty Ninth Parallel, Sonnabend, Castelli, and then Mary Boone. Then down the block to O.K. Harris and Holly Solomon, and then back up the east side of West Broadway, up to Prince and over towards "Big Castelli" and over towards Metro Pictures. On our way over there, we would stop, and lining up just the way we did at all the other galleries, file into Dean & Deluca to look at the vegetables and cakes. That was what was special about the old Dean & Deluca, of course; it was the first grocery store in New York, maybe anywhere, where you went primarily to *look* at the sublime spectacle that is food.

Only very occasionally would we actually buy something: an apple, all the way from Washington State; a bag of Mount Rainier cherries; a jar of French jam. Once, we bought a hydroponic tomato, took it home and marinated it; that was our dinner.

Mostly, though, we just looked, and that looking had lots of meaning. There was the simple pleasure of seeing old puritanical taboos broken. As you looked at the minimalist frosting on the cakes, or the warmth of color that united the green beans and the shallots and the chanterelles, you felt that you could love art, and you could love life, and never have to choose. It was the same domesticated hedonism — the same kind of scaled-down, affectionate gaze — that informed the best painting of the period — Jennifer Bartlett's or Elizabeth Murray's. And we loved to look at food because it seemed like the one area of luxury that we could ever really hope to master. Deprived of the possibilities of real possession — or for that of really big-time, sports-car-and-penthouse, sybaritism — we thought that at least we could become connoisseurs of the immaculate sensation, subtle in jellies and wise in muffins.

A couple of years later, after we actually lucked out and moved into Soho (just as it was passing the yardarm, of course), we were able to measure how much money we had by how much we could afford to buy at Dean & Deluca. What we actually did buy was, now that I think about it, pretty mundane stuff: muffins, raisins, pumpernickels, ham, bacon, coffee. Nothing you couldn't have found at a Grand Union, really; nothing, come to think of it, that ought to loom so large, so symbolically, in a fulfilled life. But shopping at Dean & Deluca gave us pleasure, and a sense of belonging to a Cultural Moment . . . a thing with a shape.

For me, the high-water mark of that era will always be the day of the Great Hurricane of 1985. My wife and I had come on a Thursday night to find the papers and the TV stations full of dire warnings about a hurricane, right on its way. It was in Georgia, it was coming up the coast, it was heading for Long Island, it would be here in the morning. Tape up your windows, they told us, fill up your bathtubs, get in enough "foodstuffs" and "canned goods" (the only time I have heard those terms used conversationally) to see you through the post-hurricane era. (Everyone in Soho actually did those things; not a window in the neighborhood was left without a Greek Orthodox cross of beige and black electrical tape.)

By Friday morning, we were in a bit of a panic. The rain had started to come down, it really seemed as though the hurricane was on its way. What *about* those canned goods? So we decided to run out to Dean & Deluca before the hurricane descended, and buy enough things in cans to eat for a few days, that is, for the storm's duration.

As we walked up towards the store, the wind picked up a little. "Buy things in jars, not cans," a neo-expressionist de-clared when we got to the store; they had all the authority in those days. We just panicked and grabbed the first things we could find: canned anchovy paste, tins of rosemary and thyme, pickled garlic.

By the time we got out of the store, it was raining — a solid New York shower. The rain soaked our bag, already unusually heavy with all those cans and jars, and, just across the street from our building, the bag broke. The bottom fell right out, and all the little silver canisters of herbs began to roll out down Broome Street, toward the Holland Tunnel. We had to chase down each one, genuinely afraid — what would happen to us if we lost all our cans? My wife ended up on the steps of our building, her arms filled with cans, while I ran up and down the street collecting the rest.

Of course, as everyone remembers, about five minutes later, the sun broke through the clouds and the hurricane was over. That had been it — we had been out in it! Lived through it — chased *cans* through it. Gone shopping at its height!

New York, which for so many of us becomes the whole world — life itself — can seem so large and abundant that what E. H. Gombrich calls the "etcetera principle" begins to oper-ate here. That's the principle at the heart of Impressionist painting, the psychological principle that started all of this — modern painting, Soho, grocery stores for artists. If you draw one tree in the foreground, and then just make a lot of dabs behind it, the human eye thinks, Oh, that tree belongs to a world — it must be one of many trees — and interprets the surrounding dabs of paint as meaningful form, other trees. We make the same mistakes with our hearts, arriving in New York, as we make with our eyes looking at Monet. We think: "Oh, I like this thing, and this thing I like is only one of many things that I am going to like that are just like it." We think, "I like to go to jazz clubs," or "I like to go to a Broadway show," or "I like special grocery stores," and it is only long after that we realize that the things we fall in love with here are unique, just like things back home. I realize now that I don't like jazz clubs; I liked listening to Ellis Larkins play at the Old Carnegie Tavern (gone now). I don't really enjoy Broadway theater much: what I liked was the forgotten revival of *Brigadoon* that played for about six weeks in 1979. And I don't much care for "gourmet" groceries; what I liked was buying a single hydro-ponic tomato at Dean & Deluca on Prince Street, on Saturday afternoon in the fall of 1981. What I like is not, as I once thought, these *kind* of things, but these *particular things*, and in New York particular things hang around just long enough for you to love them, and then they move. ◖

OLD NEW YORK postcard photographs of horse and carriage making their way on a winter's night around the circle of the Plaza Hotel. Men with cigars at the bar of Delmonico's; the upper classes dressed for an evening at the opera house on, was it? Irving Place; the tenements of the Lower East Side and the somber, black eyes of the girls at their piecework. A record for the sentiments, bittersweet moments caught by cameras still unassertive. For those of us living now, Old New York lies before the time the new Gilded-Age towers went up on Fifth Avenue. (Too much cholesterol, the cynic might observe.) Or, in an antiquarian frame of mind, we might place Old New York before the completion of the World Trade Center, the tallest building in the world for one year. One year. The statistical competitiveness of our architectural landscape admits the pharaonic nature of our dreams; floor by floor rising on the east and west rivers of Manhattan, the Niles of the new world capital, and our aluminum feluccas nestling at the 79th Street marina on the Hudson. Kennedy Airport, a sort of Ellis Island for contemporary international migrations, was only a few decades ago named Idlewild, a bit of rustic nostalgia even then. Marianne Moore, longtime resident in Brooklyn, composed a poem with "New York" as the title. The first line is "the savage's romance" and the last is a phrase in quotation, "'accessibility to experience.'" Yes, we might now and then, in imagination, find ourselves with Verrazano paddling onto the astonishing shores with a wary curiosity, meeting the native fur-traders in their "tepees of ermine" — and that perhaps would be Park Avenue. A certain wariness. We know that well here in the city where the conundrum of history has brought suddenly, overnight it seems, the aspect of a transformation quite Asiatic, bringing to mind that other great port and gateway, Bombay. But Manhattan is not suitable to, or perhaps not yet accustomed to, the ancient torpor of the long, long bereft, to the immovable forever remaining. The florid majesty of the city is designed for speed and spendthrift spectacle, for the rule of the provisional, the

Old New York

Remembering the city

in the way it was and in the way

in which it changes

ELIZABETH

HARDWICK

triumph of the transitory. The ancient promise of New York was absorption, transfiguration, or, at the least, amelioration of previous circumstance. The old streets between the rivers were the object of desire, and even now migrations continue, over the border, away from the unpromising states and countries to the south of us, the flight still and now to escape the torments of paralysis and stagnation. But the new people will have entered the Income City and the comfortable old homesteaders are cantankerous and suspicious as the family dog. A roar of chagrin and complaint fills the air with the din of a kind of intrusive suburbanism, the demand for street-pride and homogeneity. A great city of resentful inhabitants, themselves not suffering, is a slough of dreariness and repetition. Inert incompatibility, a relish for grievance, the withering of the social imagination. The Mayor instructs the citizens not to give to beggars, the reason for this institutionalizing of indifference being that there are suddenly so many of them. Yet it must be said the uniqueness of New York among the famed world cities remains: here it is always the present tense. The drift of the metropolis is not to overthrow the past but to overthrow the future before it arrives, to prevent stasis. We live in an overbuilt landscape that is nevertheless in a manic mood more appropriate to underdevelopment. Thus we must be newly "developing" what was, in terms of history, only recently created. The newest destroys and then is itself renewed. When the Trump Tower was rising on Fifth Avenue many lamented the obliteration of irreplaceable objects of antiquity, the Art Deco ornamentation of the late 1920s building going down. So, Old New York is yesterday. City-lovers, hold fast to your memories, the Indian-head pennies of "tradition." While you have turned your back, gone away for a vacation, a stunning alteration, more than one, will have taken place. The greengrocer will have packed up and moved to another site. The clever tradesman's estimation of the bottom line. But no matter. So rapid is the adjustment that the cobbler remaining in his tiny, street-front closet is a pleasurable grounding of the senses. His place is not large enough for exchange of function and so he may pursue his anachronistic craft until the entire building goes down — next summer to be sure.

A Little Etiology of Oz

Of all the cities described in words and composed in words and ambitions BY DAVE HICKEY

the evolution of cultural iconography it's a long journey from the natural to the urban "sublime," from Walden Pond to World Trade Center, if you will, but, by disregarding the rather prosaic fact of both pond and tower, we have managed to make it and live today among the double-negative spaces of the citadel of information. It is a world of shimmering Augustinian abstraction, but the most interesting view from this new City of God (where the physical world is utilized only to subdivide its myriad universes of discourse) is that of the spectacle of the "second fall of nature."

The "first fall," of course, when the God of Genesis exiled man and woman from Eden, rendered nature inaccessible and inarticulate to them, and offered in its place a world of the Word, of "pure" culture, an urban ideal of thought and law that remained intact for nearly twenty centuries until the simultaneous rise of empirical science and discovery of the New World momentarily redeemed both man and nature. The New Science apparently delivered unto him the New Eden but it was only a few centuries before the Olympians of modern physics reconceived a world not too different from that of the God of Moses. In Wallace Stevens' phrase, it was "a description without a place" — "a world of words to the end of it, in which nothing solid is its solid self," in which the objective world of "artifact" and "nature" is redefined as "commodity" and "real estate" and the Renaissance dialectic of subject and object simply dissolves into cultural hegemony.

If I had to mark the American chronological place, the watershed instant, for this profound sea change in cultural iconography, I would choose that moment when Judy Garland as Dorothy Gail emerges from her grisaille prairie bungalow into Technicolor Oz and, gazing about her at the exotic flora and fauna of Munchkinland, confides in her dog Toto her suspicion that they have somehow transcended Kansas. This moment stands as emblem for a revolution in the hierarchy of the American Dream — that moment at which the New Eden of the North American continent falls from metaphysical grace — as it had fallen from actual grace into a cloud of dust, with the withdrawal of the benediction of rain. And, conversely (as American Nature took on the biblical as well as the factual characteristics of the Wasteland), the American city, so long equated with Babylon, became, at last, the locus of wonder, taking on the trappings of Oz, the Emerald City of joyous permission.

This allegorical emblem of urban possibility in *The Wizard of Oz* finds its metaphorical precursor in Scott Fitzgerald's parable of Gatsby's green light, in which, in a moment of longing, Fitzgerald's Faustian bootlegger transposes the vision of wonder experienced by the first Dutch sailors confronting the American Eden into an equally transcendental vision of cosmopolitan capitalism symbolized by the green light at the end of the dock before Daisy Buchanan's Long Island estate.

So now we live in this new City of the Word. But even as it begins to transform itself from Romantic Ideal into Mythological Olympus, the inarticulate virus of fallen nature, remote, irrelevant and alien, begins to reassert itself, as acute somewhere in the Yucatán, the jungle and real time continue to reclaim the elegant craft and wonderful idea of a Mayan calendar. ✍

WHEN WAS IT THAT WE FIRST

discovered how forlorn we all were, how destitute we had become by the impossibility of anything like a real or divine townsmanship, and how essential was the hopelessness that perennially, and now forever, would mark even our happiest wanderings with trembling and exile? When was it that we first realized how only by cunning, wit, or stealth could

anything like citizenhood be attained, and that even this could hope to fill no more than the briefest moment: that catastrophic instant in which the quake of laughter, horror, plenitude or revenge is tracelessly consumed? When did man finally discover among all the other possible ones, that singular and unique modality that would permit him to inhabit things, even those things which since the time of Babel, he was clearly never meant to inhabit: that agency or *affectus* by which men and women in defiance of false mathematics and blind and popular philosophies, have continued nonetheless to peregrinate in cities and to mingle their very bodies within it: the indelible, revolutionary, and magnetic force of delirium?

For where else could one hope to fix the origins of a "new urban landscape"?: was it not born at the very moment that reality — whether under the sovereign sign of deity, time, or percept — ceased at last to be connected in any way to Truth, when the tissue of speculation and especially *machination* emerged exuberantly into the world as Substance itself? When was it then? How long after Plato's dialectical City, after Augustine's still more beatific City of God? If I am not mistaken, it was well over a millennium later when it suddenly appeared, so formidably modern that even for us it is terrifying to behold: the zoohemic, percolating, and peripatetic London of Giordano Bruno's *Cena de la Ceneri*. For no hallucination in history was ever quite like this one, ever quite so willful or so

SANFORD
KWINTER

Delirium Praecox

A choice
between
the pathological
states
of paranoia
and
schizophrenia

grand: the Thames, Charing Cross, Whitehall, the Strand, Butcher's Row, here folded in and onto one another like intricate tributaries of occult narration to be dissolved and transformed by the Magus' mind into that fatal theater of apology for not-yet-fashionable theories like the centricity of the Sun. Elizabethan London had served here shamelessly as the host and maiden body onto whose harbors and facades were projected the coordinates of the great Copernican Heresy, only later — by the magic of Mnemosyne — to be deliriously, even wantonly, recalled. Now the Oxford Doctors (whom Bruno anyway despised) were not about to tolerate such a flagrant assault, neither that on Dame London nor the one on common sense, and Bruno hereafter was confined for protection to chambers at the Embassy of France. But it was Bruno's *Cena* that undoubtedly unleashed for the rest of time a rich new panoply of mystical places and effects that thereafter one could reasonably ask any city to render, but also, indeed, a series of practices whose temper and form could be found nowhere else but in the depths of a pure, mathematical and overspilling delirium.

The Paris of Rabelais, or Flaubert's *Sentimental Education*, the towns of Zola, Hugo, Poe, and Dickens — they all belong to this arcane tradition, though clearly none so furiously as that of Engels in his veritably possessed *Condition of the Working Class in England*, the gothic masterpiece narration of his course through the working-class district of mid-century Manchester. Here the transformation of a city (Engels' description is so terrifying, so sustained, and so hyperbolic that one fears it could only have been true) falls nothing short of a religious cosmology: it approximates, for the age of iron and cinders, the medieval infernos of Giotto and Dante. One bristles and shudders one's way through the work just as one languishes one's way through the opiate delirium of Baudelaire's more feminine Paris, past flâneur, past neurasthenic, and especially past the proud, bored, and buttoned bourgeois as they paraded pet turtles through the Parisian *Passages*. What a legacy this offered to our own century, a century for which delirium, it should be no surprise, became finally almost a commonplace, and was used, as it had to be, by the powers of State. Yet there is one work which crowns an already crowded field — of Kafkas, Musils, Calvinos, Lawrences, Chandlers, and Célines — if not in merit then certainly in unadulterated, fanatical, irrecoverable delirium: that work is Thomas Pynchon's *Gravity's Rainbow*. Now here again figures London, though no longer just a Memory Theater for radical science as in the days of the irascible Bruno, it has now become the very field of science itself! For London is forcibly now being mapped by a random rain of Nazi rockets, each linked by a brave (but inadequately conspiratorial or delirious) Poisson equation to yet another obscure series, the periodic, excited excursions of Slothrop's Harvard-educated, Pavlov-transcended sexual member. Out of the rubble of causality springs the unholy wedding of City, Artwork, and War.

The action (and the quest for clarification, after all, what else?) soon moves across the Channel to the proverbial "Zone," a vaguely urbanistic — at least in the new sense this word would have after the end of the Second World War — setting in occupied Central Europe. Here, in an access of uncontrollable novel-

What a legacy this offered to our own century, a century for which delirium, it should be no surprise, became finally almost a commonplace, and was used, as it had to be, by the powers of State.

istic delirium, Slothrop discovers no Truth beyond a spinning profusion of technical practices ("Toto, I have a feeling we're not in Kansas anymore") — film, chemistry, psychology, physics, engineering, finance — all of which focus quite insanely on him. Can the history of the twentieth century really have been written, engraved, in that very same body part where his own desire is made incarnate? Perhaps because the weight of such a densely drawn hypothesis is too much for a single person (let alone penis) to bear, Slothrop, already disintegrating, sheds his identity entirely and scatters into the gray multiplicity. Of course, Slothrop had already too well articulated the problem himself: "Either everything is connected, or else nothing is."

Now in this last sentence one may certainly discover as well the occult conditions of our own new urban landscape. Isn't it — and has it not always been? — a choice between two pathological states?: *paranoia*, that limpid delirium of collective representations, massive blocs, and sinister orchestrations; or *schizophrenia*, the fuzzy delirium of fragmentation, minutiae, and disappearance.

This essay then would like, if it could, to be dedicated to the protoliterary procession of characters who daily recast the city according to their own need and in the secret image of their own delirious cosmos, the guerrilla cartographers and microdevelopers of abstract spaces, the bottle and can gatherers, graffitists, nomad moralists with bodies racked and twisted by the syndrome of Tourette, the drifters, decalcomaniacs, the criers (Sense! they yell, as if that were not the most delirious thing of all), the hirsute laughers, the brick-in-the-box peddlers, bush planters and cack collectors, low-budget camera crews, cart pushers, traffic-island emperors — demented urbanists and hijackers all of them, yet whose sovereign delirium records the sole truth that perhaps our cities today are capable of producing. ⚑

YEARS AGO

WHEN THE COUNTRY WAS MORE OPTIMISTIC, LE CORBUSIER WENT TO INDIA TO DESIGN HIS MODEL MODERN CITY, AND IN THE MIDDLE OF THAT CITY HE PLACED A MONUMENTAL SCULPTURE OF "THE OPEN HAND," HIS SYMBOL OF RECIPROCITY AND THE MAJESTY OF TOOLS.

In today's urban landscape a different open hand greets us — the hand of the homeless man or woman — often several times on a single block, and we are less confident that architecture offers us a solution to the kind of social problem that hand symbolizes.

Two blocks from my apartment there's a sign posted on a building: "What can you do about the homeless?" Well, what I can do first of all is try my best not to join them. I can also: give them a quarter; send in a check; raise the subject over dinner; or, since writing about architecture is how I keep a roof over my head, I even go as far as to ask how the question might apply to architects.

If you provide a homeless person with shelter, he is no longer homeless; in theory, if you create enough shelters, the problem of homelessness disappears. But architecture is not just a matter of physical shelter. Architects do not only build buildings; they also build consciousness, not only in the sense of motivating solutions to problems but also in trying to define them. To the extent that solutions depend on an understanding of causes, homelessness is a conceptual as well as a material problem. Like "mental illness," another social problem which plagues an estimated one-third of the homeless population, homelessness is a way of thinking about certain people who do not conform to social expectations. Prior to the sixteenth century, as Michel Foucault recounted, there were mad people, but the concept of mental illness awaited the emergence of reason as a governing cultural norm.

Ten years ago, many cities had "street people," a term which carried the more positive connotation of staking a claim to a part of urban space. There's nothing new about poor people, but the term homelessness defines them in a negative relation to our contemporary conception of the home — or perhaps our failure to clarify what the idea of home means to us. I once suggested that the quickest (not the best) design solution to homelessness was to install doorbells inside the door of every building in New York (a bit like smoke detectors), with the requirement that we ring them every time we go out and let the homeless — whether or not they want to — receive us. The point of the bell was to remind us of the odd nature of "public space" in a culture of private enterprise.

Many are disturbed by the "privatization" that occurred during the Reagan years, from the demands for tax credits for private education, with its implications for public schools, to the ersatz "public spaces" private developers have been encouraged to provide in zoning trade-offs for increased building size. But the problem didn't start in 1980. "The most disturbing aspect of life in the United States today," wrote James Marston Fitch in 1966, a time of national affluence, "is the widening discrepancy between privatized luxury and public amenity." Though that gap is no narrower today, an affliction of our time is that, relative to the expectations of those who grew up amid postwar abundance, we now have privatized poverty as well.

Privatization in postwar years unfolded chiefly in the suburbs (where the only "public space," apart from the highway, was the living room, symbolically cordoned off from family use), with consequences that are only now being felt. To a large extent, the city today has

48

become a "homeless shelter" even for those with homes. It is a refuge for the middle-class generation that grew up in the suburbs and was economically expelled from them when they went off to college. The yuppie lifestyle, it has been pointed out, is one of downward mobility. As Michael Kinsley observed, "affordable luxuries," like designer chocolate chip cookies, "serve as consolation for the lack of unaffordable luxuries like a large house." Or even a decent apartment.

It's arguable to what extent this suburban counter-migration has displaced the urban poor onto the streets. What isn't arguable is that this phenomenon has much to do with the way the homelessness problem has been conceptualized. The problem is not only that some have and others don't. It is that many of those who have so little have it so precariously. Many urban dwellers today who grew up surrounded by the suburbs' signs of stability and plenty now pay through the nose to share spaces only marginally better than the cardboard-box hovel in the alley. I don't mean to minimize the value of that margin and I'm not trying to drum up sympathy for yuppies. A roof over your head is not nothing. And, in fact, that is not a minor part of the role the homeless play in consciousness. Like the "Home" section in the newspaper, which does not so much report on our homes as, in effect, replace them, the homeless make it easier to accept that home can come in a box.

The visions of architects have yet to catch up to the message the homeless hold in their hands. The "solution" to homelessness lies not only in providing beds for the night, jobs and training for the unemployed, but also in the ability of architects to reconceive the home with imagery capable of persuading public and private developers to support it. Just as Frank Lloyd Wright demonstrated with the Usonian Houses that it was possible to devise a compelling image of the suburban home as an extension of the car, so architects now must configure the urban home as an extension of the appointment book, a living diary.

Partly as a consequence of eroded optimism, and of

HERBERT MUSCHAMP

Quicker Than the Eye

A CRITIC'S DIALOGUE *of the* PUBLIC *and* PRIVATE SPACE *for the* CONTEMPORARY CITY

belief in their own powers of invention, this is a conservative time which architects and developers have tried to serve by going back to old models for their ideas, giving us surface illusions of old-fashioned luxury, of pre-war residential architecture (doesn't everyone want a pre-war building in a stable neighborhood?). These buildings borrow forms from old urban architecture but in spirit they embody a wholly suburban craving for cosmetic illusions of stability and order. This direction has not been without value; it has helped restore a needed sense of continuity to a streetscape battered by decades of modern upheaval.

But in the long run it cannot be much more than a holding action, a transition leading to the emergence of a new building type that reflects with clarity the movement of our lives today. This architecture will be wholly modern in design but less disruptive to the street; flexible in building size, interior disposition, externally applied form and terms of occupancy; linked, physically or financially, to employment or profession; spare as a running outfit; a type something like a college dormitory, something like a storage warehouse, something like an SRO hotel, something like a shopping cart, an architecture that is not embarrassed but in fact jubilant to partake of what Christopher Isherwood called our "reduction of the material plane to mere symbolic convenience." The ingredients of this architecture have been around for a long time; what remains is for architects to create from them imagery sufficiently compelling to enter our consciousness of options.

The position of New York City's government is that it doesn't want to make homeless shelters "too nice" because then people will want to stay in them forever, that is, render them a home. The real danger, of course, is that any minimally livable accommodation would be indistinguishable from apartments renting for thousands a month, which would blow the illusion architects carefully orchestrate for developers that these apartments are "luxurious." Architects should be working overtime precisely to blow that illusion.

49

The city that is the world but also dissipates the world for one small place. Tropical Forests and the Urban Landscape We drive on automobile tires made from rubber from the Amazon, wash our hair with shampoo containing palm oils from Southeast Asia or hit golf balls coated with latex from Central America. How many architects are aware that many of the early designs for steel-beam architecture were based on the venation of the leaf of the giant water lily of the Northwest Amazon? MARK J. PLOTKIN

Tropical Forests are home to many species with great potential to benefit mankind, yet the majority of these plants and animals have never been examined by scientists. Nevertheless, the relatively few species that have been studied have yielded a treasure of valuable products. The rosy periwinkle from Madagascar produces our frontline drug for the treatment of childhood leukemia. The Cinchona tree from the Andes of South America is the source of quinine, important for treating malaria and cardiac arrhythmias. As many as one in twelve of our prescription drugs has been extracted from rainforest plants. A leading plant chemist recently wrote that nothing at all is known of the chemical composition of 98.6% of the Brazilian flora — and Brazil has more species of plants than any other country in the world.

Much of our agriculture is based on plants which originated in equatorial regions. Imagine a breakfast without coffee, tea, hot chocolate, cornflakes, Rice Crispies, orange juice, pineapple juice, grapefruit juice, tomato juice, or bananas and you can see how depauperate our existence would be within our urban cocoons without these tropical products. The search for new tropical products has been a driving force in Western civilization, from Marco Polo to Christopher Columbus.

In many ways, the Urban Landscape is the antithesis of the Tropical Forest. The Urban Landscape is the ultimate cocoon — we are no longer at the mercy of scorching days, freezing nights, famines, wild animals — all very real threats when our species first arose on the savannas of East Africa millions of years ago. In our cities, we have bent nature to our will — most of the trees were either planted or intentionally spared. Even the most "natural" settings — Central Park, Golden Gate Park — were shaped by the hand of man. The Urban Landscape is a universe that we created and control, but in the Tropical Forest ecosystem we are just one species among thousands.

As the Urban Landscape expands, Tropical Forests continue to contract. Every year, an area of rainforest the size of the state of New York is degraded or completely destroyed. A recent satellite photograph of the Brazilian Amazon revealed 7000 major forest fires in a single day. Given the rates of population growth in many developing countries, the outlook for some of the jungles of the world is bleak and only growing worse.

We should not, however, conserve nature in general and rainforest in particular for solely utilitarian purposes. There exist strong aesthetic, moral, and scientific reasons as well. In a world increasingly covered with asphalt and concrete, it is essential to know that wild places still exist. Basically stated, "civilized man sleeps better knowing that somewhere, in some far-off place, a tiger still roams the jungle." 🖌

Hamilton Avenue Municipal Solid Waste Incinerator (Inactive) Brooklyn, New York

A human jaw makes fine jewelry. Strung on butcher's string, beating back and forth on the breastbone of our guide. The honey teeth unalloyed in the bone gray. A tiny gold cross in a back molar that has denied the prying of fingernail, knife and ballpoint pen. Precious metals, copper and aluminum, mined from this building. Weeks of working to rip sinks from walls, pulling out the pipes earns about six dollars in change. Lidless eyes in the porcelain weep rust. Sinks levered on the floor, bowls of the dried shapings that evidence feasts on the spoilage. Over a sink a book is read with no beginning and no end, just middle pages that are torn as needed and pinched behind, others like them litter the floor, little fortune cookies of filth. There is no fear of rats here. Rooms and rooms of fires burning particle board and paper and thick slabs of the kind of tarred panels that blacken the lungs. Fires on landings, fires through the floors. Fires kept by kicking paper in or out. Surprise

52

at its creep and sudden consummation of a day's forage. A book scuffed in then reprieved by an intriguing title. Foot grates for the long gone shoes of incineration engineers are propped on cindered blocks and milk crates for cooking. Milk crate okay for two fires before folding waxen into flame. No fear of rats in this place. Tiny bones of vermin snap underfoot, brittle straw sucked clean of sweet meat and marrow nectar. Somewhere there begins a joke. How does a man. With a fused spine. There is a faltering problem with logic. A new joke begins. How does a man. With a fused spine. In a corner a cuffed hand snuffing a sleeved spark is a fistfight. Burn then, damn you. At the edge of an ashless pit a chaise lounge is folded open and woven with foam. Special care of its position, cooler nearby of possessions, a day at the beach along this black liquid shore. Jetsam, jetsam, jetsam, says a pneumatic pump somewhere in a world away. A form in long layers of street grime and a pink chiffon bathrobe fans on its back across paper shards and sheets Esther! Esther Williams! More fires, fires in the furnace room, none in

MARK

RICHARD

on the

RICH

LODE/LOAD

of the

CARNAL

DETRITUS

of the

CITY

the furnace. A step is taken from a fire, stepping around with a stick and knife. In the open hatch of a furnace a figure snores. A broken-headed dial reads thousands of degrees. Draft from the empty chimneys is cool, fresh, stoking a fire burning on its own knee-high coals etching on the ceiling a big black eye. It is time to leave the proddings of knives and stick. Out to where the sun shines on the lot of this building, where the shopping carts collect, the infernal schooners that rattle our streets with plastic sheets of sail. Time to get outside where the carts are bunched cart into cart from markets citywide, wheels worn, woven with smart pennants from political rallies and playing fields, carts chained against thieves, carts too wide to ply the iron bar barricades to this place. Get out the crooked crawlspace that is narrow and bright with wear at shopping-cart level where some spend dark hours trying to fight the fit, dragging the things in behind them. Escape at the end, how does a man with spinal fusion look up at the Empire State? With eyes rolled to the top of the head, jaw dropped in laughter that betrays the gold inside. ▰

THE EXHIBITION

Twenty-eight works by **Vito Acconci, Dennis Adams/ Andrea Blum, Kim Adams, Judith Barry, Alan Belcher, Dan Graham, Susan Hiller, Hodgetts + Fung, Henry Jesionka, Kristin Jones and Andrew Ginzel, Michael Kalil, Kawamata, Jon Kessler, Kunst Brothers, Justen Ladda, Morphosis, Matt Mullican, Jean Nouvel, Joel Otterson, Nam June Paik, Liz Phillips, Robert Price, Martha Schwartz, Haim Steinbach, Mierle Laderman Ukeles, Jacques Vieille, Richard Wentworth, and Stephen Willats**
Video by **MICA-TV** *Photographed by* **Jon Abbott**

Garden with Fountain, 1988 **Vito Acconci** **(b. 1940), American** Junk cars, concrete, water, plants *Courtesy of Barbe*

56

Landfill: Bus Station, 1988

Dennis Adams
(b. 1948), American

Andrea Blum
(b. 1950), American

Cast concrete, steel, fluorescent light, Plexiglas, Duratrans, photograph (Selwyn Tait, "East Cape Funeral, South Africa," 1985, © Blackstar Agency)

58

A, RESISTANT

ADVERTISING.

H WILL STAGE A

, IMPLICATING

TICS OF THE

Chameleon Unit, 1988

Kim Adams (b. 1951), Canadian

Sleepers, tractor cab, painted steel, wood

Courtesy of Galerie Christiane Chassay, Montreal

61

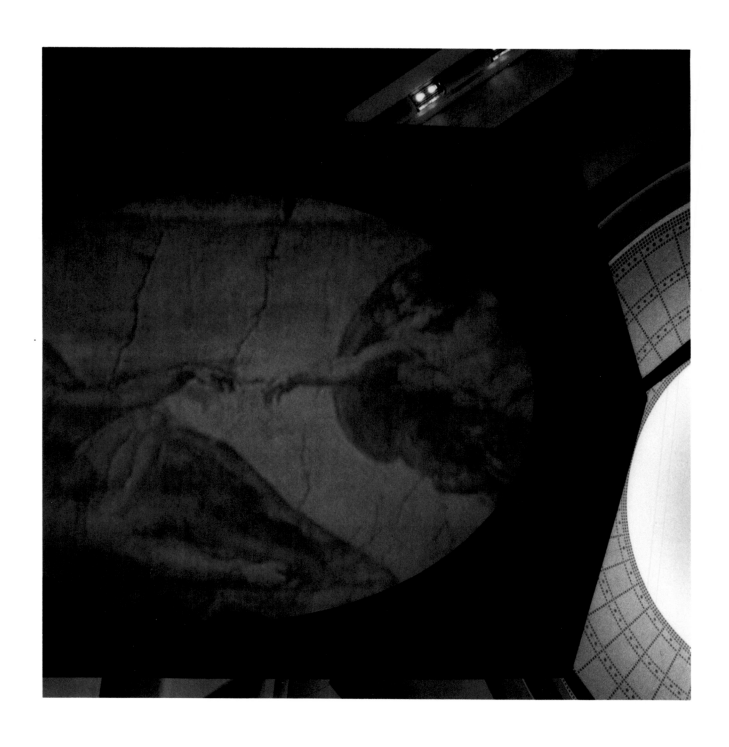

Adam's Wish, 1988 **Judith Barry** **(b. 1949), American** Video projection

Office Complex '88, 1988 **Alan Belcher** (b. 1957), **Canadian** Color lamine photographs, bricks, Velcro *Courtesy of*

Triangular Structure with Two-Way Mirror Sliding Door, 1988

Dan Graham (b. 1942), American

Brushed aluminum framework, laminated glass and
laminated two-way mirrored glass over existing window
glass

Courtesy of Marian Goodman Gallery

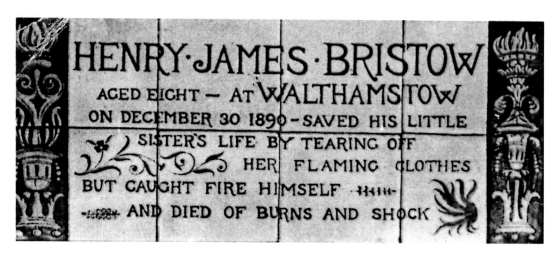

Monument, 1981-1988

Susan Hiller (b. 1942), American

39 C-type photographs, audiotape, park bench

Courtesy of Pat Hearn Gallery

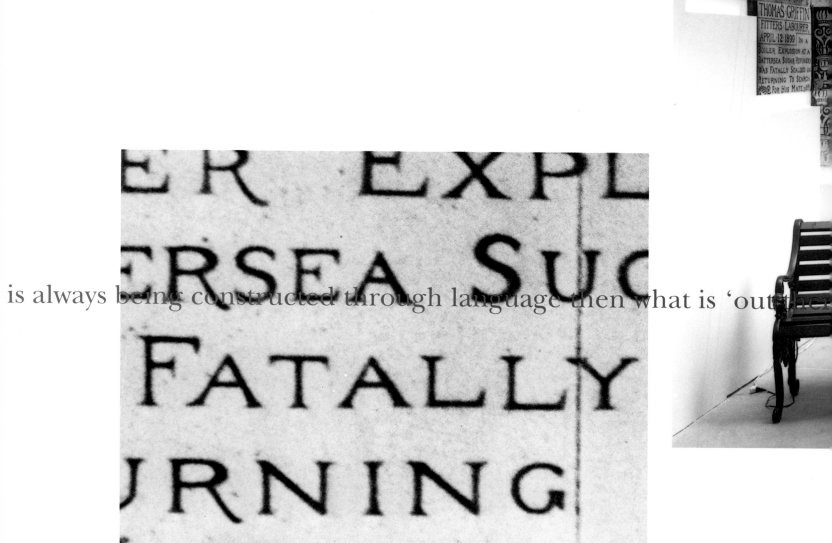

is always being constructed through language then what is 'out there

the same as what is 'inside'. This is how the dead speak to us and thr

Near Things, 1988

Hodgetts + Fung

Craig Hodgetts (b. 1937), American

Hsin-Ming Fung (b.1953), American

Concrete blocks and mixed media

Nullstadt, 1988 **Henry Jesionka** **(b. 1957), Canadian** Optical system, laser-based seismograph

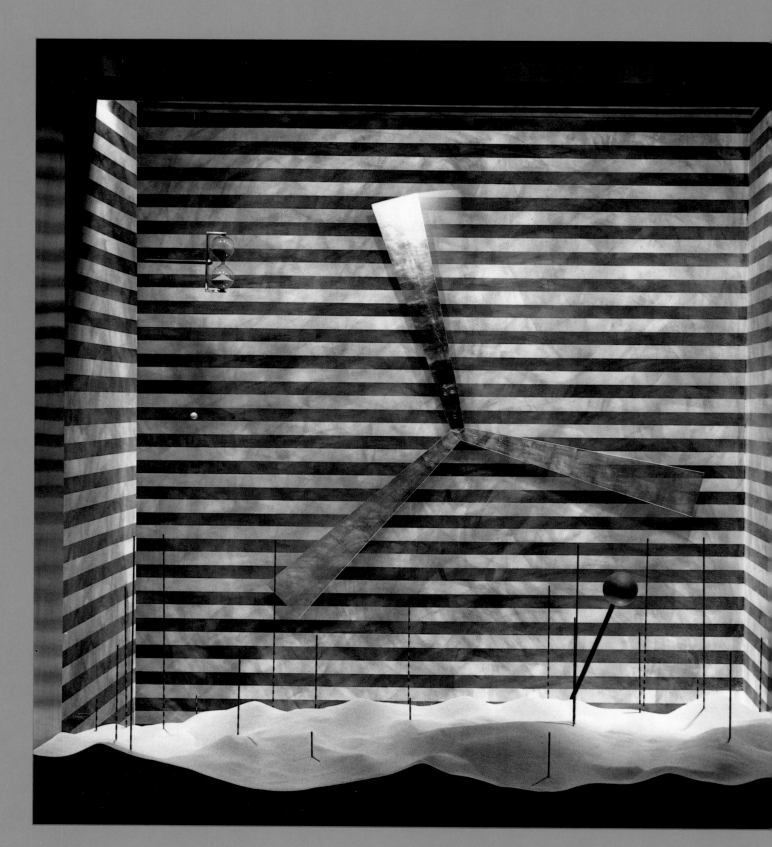

Geotaxis, 1988

Kristin Jones

(b. 1956), American

Andrew Ginzel

(b.1954), American

Silica, aluminum, calcium carbonate, wood, steel, paint,

pigment, copper, gold

Courtesy of Barbara Flynn Gallery

Elysian Field III A, 1988 **Michael Kalil (b. 1944), American** Mixed media — space and light

78

Favela in Battery Park City: Inside/Outside, 1988

Tadashi Kawamata

(b. 1953), Japanese

Wood

79

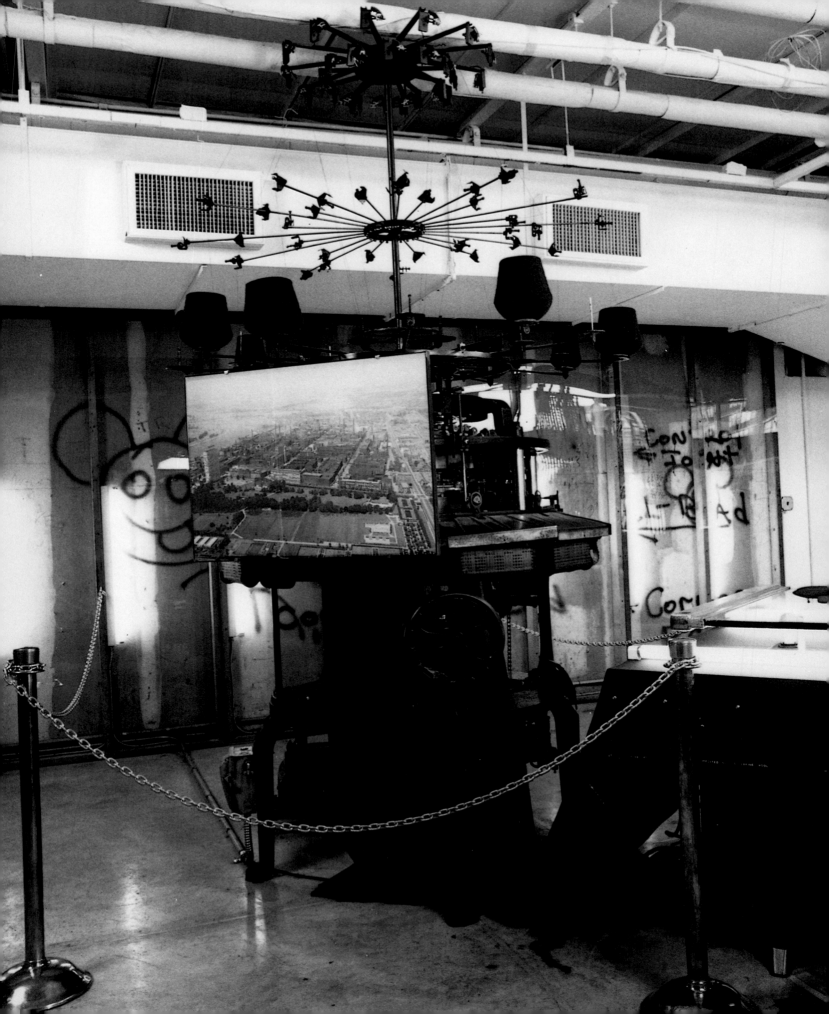

Exodus, 1988

Jon Kessler (b. 1957), American

Mixed media

Courtesy of Luhring Augustine Gallery

Volta/Votive, 1988

Kunst Brothers (b. 1987)

Alison Saar (b. 1956), American

Tom Leeser (b. 1956), American

Car batteries, sand, video

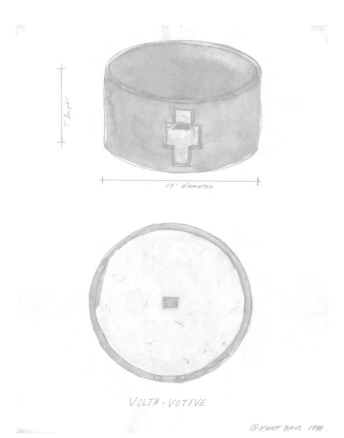

83

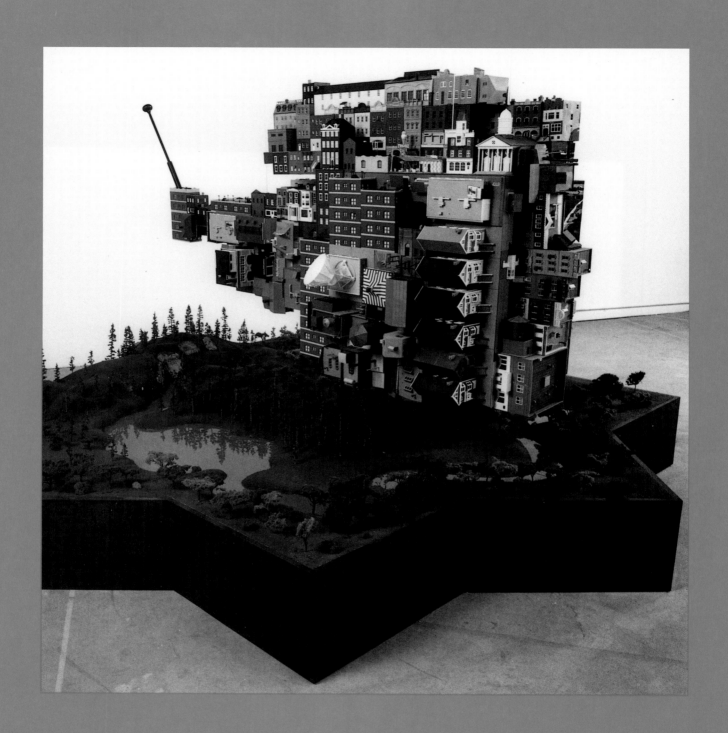

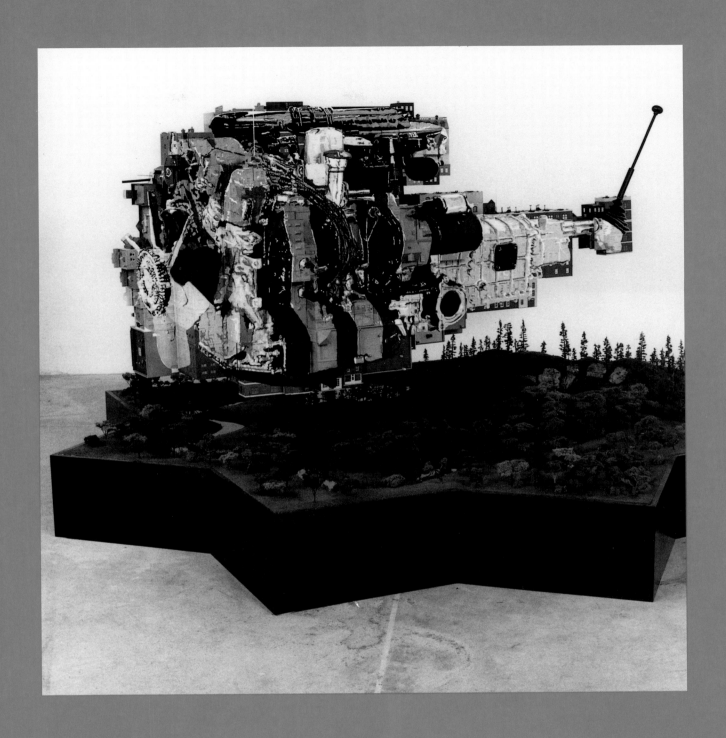

Romeo and Juliet, 1988 **Justen Ladda** **(b. 1953), German** Mixed media

85

Room Compressed, 1988

Morphosis

Thom Mayne (b. 1944), American

Michael Rotondi (b. 1949), American

Steel, wood, plant materials, various building materials

Created in collaboration with Russ Drinker + Scott Marble

Associates

Untitled, 1988 **Matt Mullican** **(b. 1951), American** Nylon banner *Courtesy of Michael Klein, Inc.*

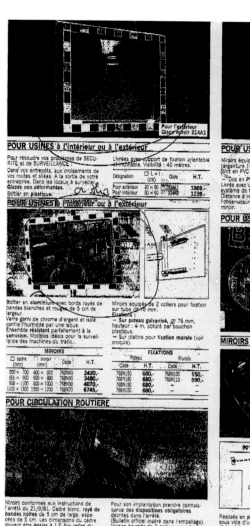

Ecosystem, 1988

Jean Nouvel (b. 1945), French

Mixed media

The Cage (The Living Room), 1988 **Joel Otterson** (b. 1959), **American** Steel, copper, galvanized steel, glass, chicken

antique Dutch ceramic tiles, porcelain Italian lamps with quartz bulbs *Courtesy of Jay Gorney Modern Art*

Ruin, 1988

Nam June Paik

(b. 1932), American

Video sculpture with 24 monitors and 45 antique television

cabinets

Courtesy of Carl Solway Gallery, Cincinnati, Ohio

FLOORPLAN FOR CYMBAL   SCALE: 1/4" = 1'

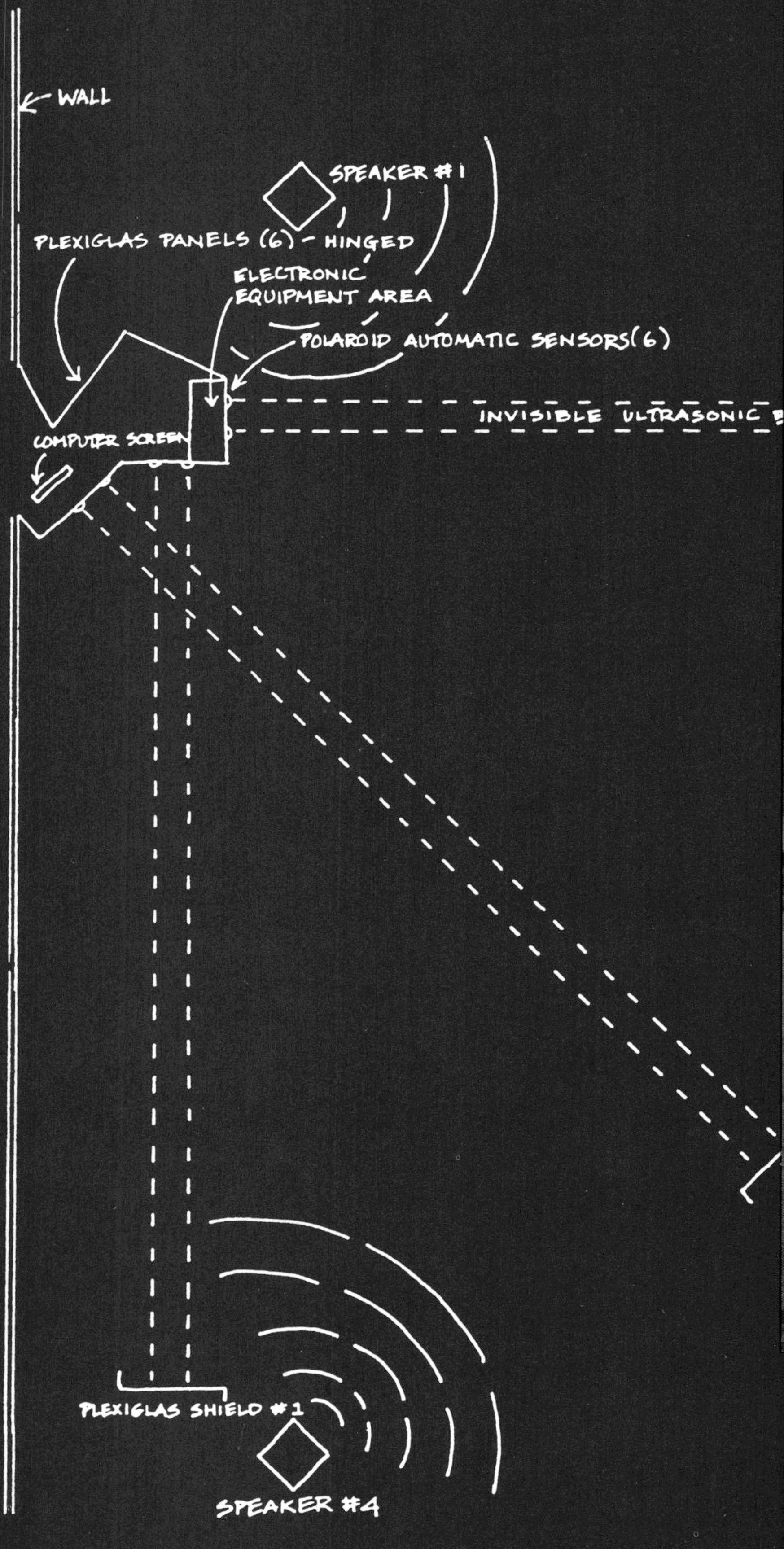

← WALL

SPEAKER #1

PLEXIGLAS PANELS (6) - HINGED

ELECTRONIC
EQUIPMENT AREA

POLAROID AUTOMATIC SENSORS (6)

INVISIBLE ULTRASONIC

COMPUTER SCREEN

PLEXIGLAS SHIELD #1

SPEAKER #4

SPEAKER #3

Cymbal, 1985 **Liz Phillips** **(b. 1951), American** Sound equipment

face \fas\ *n* 1 : the fro
head 2 : PRESENCE ⟨in t
ger⟩ 3 : facial expression
sad ∼ on⟩ 4 : GRIMAC
5 : outward appearance ⟨
the ∼ of it⟩ 6 : BOLDNESS
PRESTIGE ⟨afraid to lose
surface of something; *esp*
principal surface   face
— face·less *adj*   face
²face *vb* faced; fac·ing
front brazenly 2 : to line
esp. with a different mate
cover the front or surface
ing with marble⟩ 3 : to
face ⟨*faced* him with the
stand or sit with the face t
sun⟩ 5 : to front on ⟨a
the park⟩ 6 : to oppose
up to his foe⟩ 7 : to tu
body in a specified direc

Face, 1988

Robert Price (b. 1950), American

Screen printing on aluminum veneer, wood and lacquer

Courtesy of Cable Gallery

99

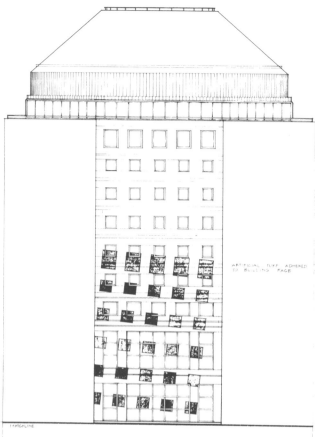

Turf Parterre Garden, 1988

Martha Schwartz

(b. 1950), American

Artificial turf and removed sod

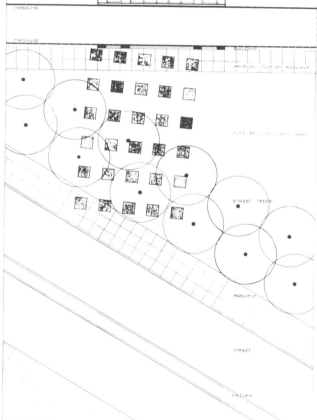

Adirondack Tableau, 1988

Haim Steinbach

(b. 1944), American

Wood and owls

Courtesy of Sonnabend Gallery and Jay Gorney Modern Art

103

Ceremonial Arch Honoring Service Workers in the New Service Economy, 1988

Mierle Laderman Ukeles (b. 1939), American

Worn-out workgloves donated by workers from twelve different services, work lights and various service-specific materials

Courtesy of Ronald Feldman Gallery

14 Arborvitae, 1986-1988 **Jacques Vieille** **(b. 1948), French** Wood, plants, buckets

Neighbour, Neighbour, 1988

Richard Wentworth

(b. 1947), British

Milled steel, cork, cable

Courtesy: Lisson Gallery, London, and Wolff Gallery, New York

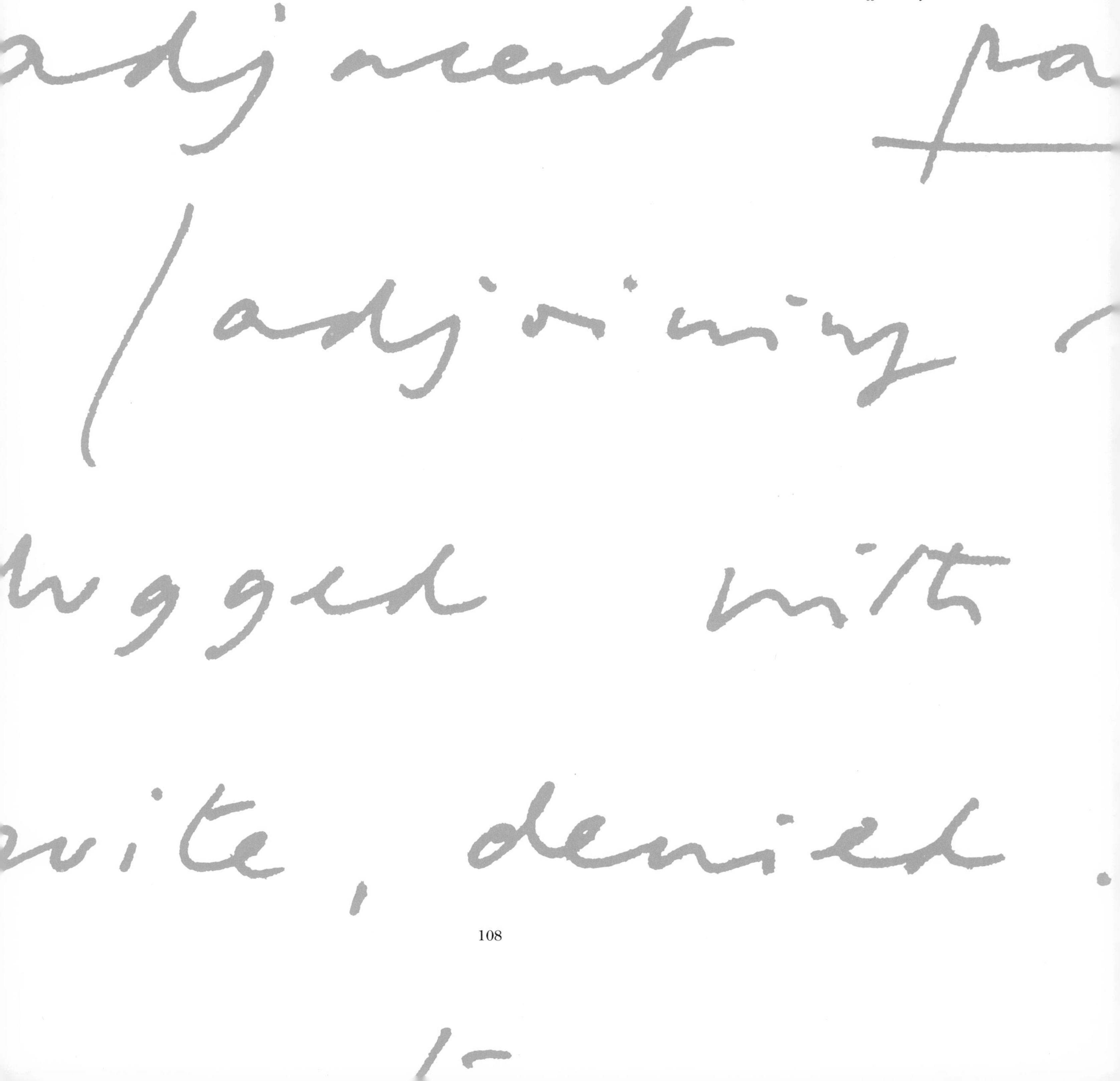

adjacent

(adjoining

lugged   with

vite, denied .

THE NEW URBAN LANDSCAPE

An exhibition of installations by artists and architects on issues of contemporary city life

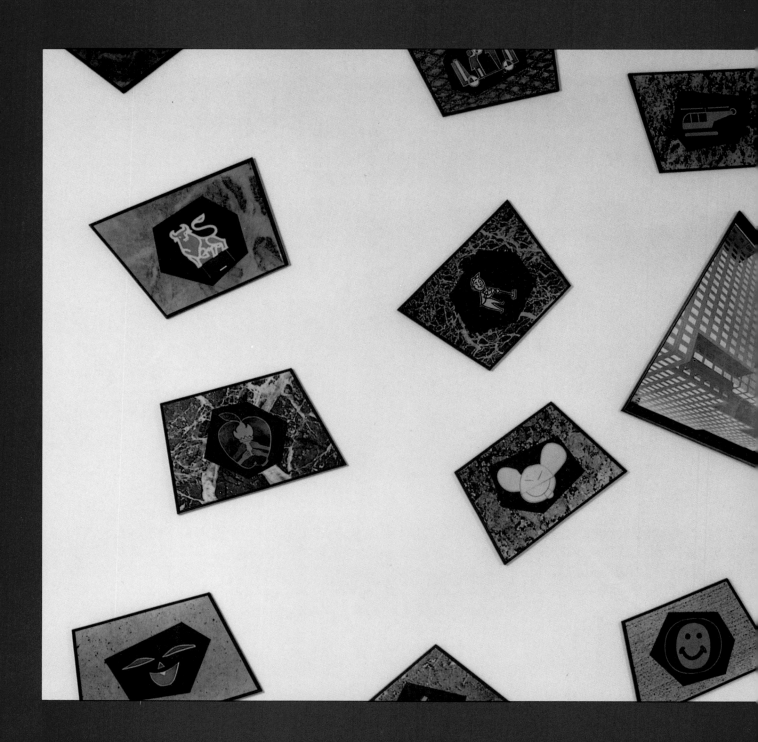

Signs and Messages from Corporate America, 1988 **Stephen Willats** **(b. 1943), British** Photographic pri

...otographic dyes, paint, mounting board, mounting paper, wood, frames and audiovisual equipment *Courtesy of Lisson Gallery, London*

The New Urban Landscape, 1988

MICA-TV

Carole Ann Klonarides (b. 1951), American

Michael Owen (b. 1952), American

Videotape

NATURE & CULTURE

Jon Kess

Michael Kalil
Space Engineer

RDING TO INSTRUCTION

With characteristic humor, **Vito Acconci** has installed two sets of automobiles on either side of a large pane of glass and encased them in concrete in *Garden with Fountain*. Rearing like horses in public sculpture of an earlier era, water spews from the hood of a car on the outside of the glass in a vain attempt to nourish the plants sprouting from the inside of the cars. The work addresses the adversarial role of urban development in relationship to the natural world and illustrates nature's struggle to assert itself. The paradoxical aspects of this conflict are represented by the automobile itself: a useful harnessing of energy and an aural and air pollutant; a private convenience and a public nuisance; an efficient tool and potential weapon; a sleek, moving sculpture and an eyesore.

Landfill: Bus Station by **Dennis Adams** and **Andrea Blum** transforms an ordinary and functional object — a bus stop — into a site for social commentary. Bus stop signage, which usually takes the form of appealing advertisement, presents surprising information in this case. An oversize image of a South African funeral is penetrated at an acute angle by a concrete bench. The similar shapes of the bench and the casket, as well as the fact that all elements are off-kilter, activate a drama in which the bus patron plays an implicit role. The material, color and weight of the structure extend the somber metaphor, inserting thought-provoking substance into an everyday context.

Canadian artist **Kim Adams'** *Chameleon Unit* responds to the urban dilemma of restricted space and limited housing and the need for inventive, even humorous solutions to big problems. Adams constructs a multipurpose van out of available materials, providing spaces for work, home and leisure functions. Truck body parts and agricultural farm equipment are ingeniously recycled in Adams' compact design, conspicuously equipping *Chameleon Unit* with an entertainment center, an essential part of '80s life-style and values. Adams writes of his "interest... in models for mobile urban dwellings, which combine the function of vehicle and home or office space in one transportable unit." In this work, not only does he gently satirize the way we live by suggesting a solution to the problem of too-little space, but he also emphasizes the mobility which characterizes and to some extent drives behavior in our society.

Judith Barry utilizes modern technology to comment on the cultural history of cities in her video installation *Adam's Wish*. Computerized editing techniques make it possible for her to juxtapose and overlay images from history with modern counterparts and intermix still frames with live action. Her piece centers on a detail of Michaelangelo's Sistine Ceiling in which Adam languidly reaches out to God to receive the life force. Barry's fast-moving and funny visual poem interprets humankind's subsequent fall from grace. Her imagery includes both classical and contemporary domed buildings with which people attempt to encapsulize authority, grandeur and even spirituality. Barry focuses on the ways in which architecture embodies our goals and values. Installed in the domed entrance foyer to The World Financial Center, Barry's work allows the viewer valuable insights into how architecture reveals the way a culture perceives itself.

ANY
QUESTIONS

EXPLANATORY
NOTES
on the
EXHIBITION
by **PHILIP
YENAWINE**
*Director of Education
Museum of Modern Art
New York*

In his sculptural photo-object *Office Complex '88,* **Alan Belcher** has constructed an elliptical concrete block wall, which is then wrapped with an immense photo enlargement of an office building under construction. The photographs serve as a facade for the cinder-block construction while simultaneously depicting the internal skeleton of an office structure. This imposing and colorful object can be read as a photo mural of a slice of city life, ironically supported and framed by construction materials. And it can also be seen as sculpture which has almost become architecture, complete with high-tech, modernistic graffiti. The work sets up a series of paradoxical relationships which not only focus on structure as subject and substance of both art and architecture, but also heighten awareness of image and object, surface and support, form and space.

Dan Graham deals with the perception of visual information in his *Triangular Structure with Two-Way Mirror Sliding Door*. The exterior of this tiny triangular room, created by a two-way mirror encased in a metal frame, reflects the environment of moving people, sunlight, clouds, etc., and structurally mirrors the framing of the building's glass facade as well. Inspired by the ubiquitous glass and metal grids of the urban landscape, Graham's angular insertion catches the passerby unaware both because of the unpredicted reflection and because it interrupts the squared corner. Inside the space, the viewer can look outward to watch other viewers who can't see them, but also becomes a kind of caged display, visible from inside the building's foyer.

Simply titled *Monument,* **Susan Hiller's** installation is an homage to the citizenry of the City of London. Hiller has enlarged photographs of headstones in a London cemetery and installed them in a cross formation. The photographs of actual memorial plaques describe in graphic and melodramatic terms the heroic circumstances of each victim's demise. The viewer is invited to sit on a bench and listen through headphones to the artist as she describes ideas about heroism, martyrdom, and the nature of life and death. *Monument* not only pays homage to "everyday heroes," but also asks us to question the cultural tradition of monuments and what virtues dictate their worthiness.

In *Near Things,* **Craig Hodgetts** and **Hsin-Ming Fung** express the sometimes ironic relationship between human activity and the processes of nature. Each of the five columns or structures called "shrines" involves a series of contraptions which juxtapose natural elements – water, earth, ice, tar and grass – with man-made facsimiles. That we can and in fact do imitate nature, through such actions as freezing, is incorporated within the pieces, which document as well our attempts to control nature and the great lengths we will go to do so. The source of amusement in this work is provided by samples of such phenomena as Astroturf and other useful but somewhat ridiculous results of our efforts. Implicit in the work is the price paid by reliance on technology to replace what we ignore or destroy in our relentless quest for dominion.

In *Nullstadt* (German for "no city"), **Henry Jesionka** builds a room alongside a window wall of the exhibition space, insetting lenses which allow light to penetrate and project onto other walls, floor and ceiling of the room, operating much like a camera obscura. The lenses are filled with water and therefore distort the scale and color of the projected images of the plaza, river and landscape outside. While being asked to decipher the projections, the viewer's movements also trigger a red laser beam which seems to lace the individual into the locale. "No city" deflates the idea of the city as a permanent and fixed place, and underscores the concept of the city as a site of process and transaction inhabited by individuals.

Kristin Jones and **Andrew Ginzel** deal with time and change in their installation called *Geotaxis,* which refers to the effects of gravity on the environment. The viewer looks into a kind of enclosed display unit, much like a museum diorama, in which there is a very carefully crafted and continuously changing "landscape" of sand and light. In the work, the sand keeps pouring in and also sifting out, drifting in various configurations alternately revealing and hiding objects placed in the window. An hourglass and a gold metronome mark the passage of time in this surreal world, giving a sense of fast-motion evolution, a quick process of growth and decay.

Michael Kalil uses technology to reassess the relationship between people and their environment in *Elysian Field III A.* The viewer looks into an enclosed chamber which simulates, through manipulation of light and space, a weightless or zero-gravity atmosphere. This sensation alters the nature of space and movement and replaces the earthly phenomenon of gravity with another sense of order. Kalil projects our expectations into another context in order to encourage us to think about "man's intrinsic relationship to the earth."

Tadashi Kawamata's inspiration for *Favela in Battery Park City: Inside/Outside* comes specifically from the slum dwellings in South America called *favelas* – shelters which are built of scrap materials and makeshift methods. Using similar materials and construction techniques, *Inside/Outside* contrasts the human scale, personality and immediacy of such temporary structures with the sophistication and high technology of modern corporate architecture. The metaphorized title, as well as the placing of the structure (half inside, half outside the building), suggests we think about barriers and disparities, as between the rich and the poor in our society. Kawamata's work raises large questions specifically about the role architecture plays in maintaining social stratifications. It also functions as sculpture, being equally a pattern of lines, shapes, colors, solids and voids — a visual object to be explored.

Jon Kessler's *Exodus* employs a large antiquated knitting machine combed with elements of recent technology including a computer and the accoutrements of offices (desk, fluorescent lights, glass doors and speaker phone). In so doing, he creates a paradigm for the city infrastructure, and also a fabulous Rube Goldberg–like "gadget" as individual and idiosyncratic as the references to mass society seem anonymous. The tables approaching the knitting machine take the form of an assembly line (as well as an airport runway) for the production of the traditional gray flannel suit. Together these elements function as a mechanized representation of various systems of communication and mass production which drive the city's economic and social structure. The computer and telephone systems that Kessler incorporates into the work are used in such a way as to represent, in the artist's words, "communication falling in on itself" and the alienation that is part and parcel of the age of technology.

In a gesture of ironic humor, the **Kunst Brothers** in *Volta/Votive* have constructed a building of old car batteries for this exhibition in a building which adjoins Battery Park. They filled the structure with sand scattered with artifacts of the cultural and historic past, just as the land beneath The World Financial Center was created from an immense landfill project in what was once the Hudson River. Set in a dramatically darkened space, the structure further refers to historical antecedents by taking its circular form from a portion of Castle Clinton, which guarded New York Harbor from the time of early Dutch settlements; it is also intended to refer to ceremonial sites of earlier Native Americans. The negatives and positives of development as well as electrical current are suggested – and the visual pun extended – by the use of plus and minus signs for door and window.

The encroachment of urban life on natural landscapes is the theme of **Justen Ladda's** *Romeo and Juliet.* The title, which evokes Shakespeare's star-crossed lovers, refers equally to our troubled romance with nature: we simultaneously idealize it even as we develop and destroy it. In Ladda's sculpture a simulated car engine, made up of plastic models of buildings, hovers over a perfect pastoral scene. The engine and landscape represent two powerful polarities locked in a precarious and sensitive balance. As Ladda states, the concept of "transgression and death" is an integral part of the work.

The architectural team of **Morphosis** addresses the issue of space in urban development with their work *Room Compressed.* Using raw building materials, Morphosis has built a lumber and steel structure in the center of the South End Avenue cul-de-sac. The dynamics of the work are created by the relationship of the circular motion of

traffic and the series of sprockets, pistons and ropes that appear to ultimately compress the tree within the sculpture. The caged space implies both the sense of confinement and compression found in denser urban settings. The tree, symbolizing nature, is both a victim and a survivor.

Matt Mullican's huge, heraldic banner uses a series of symbols which effectively unite the themes and essential ideas in *The New Urban Landscape.* Mullican divides the banner into four squares, each containing symbols which represent (clockwise from bottom left) the world, the sign (outward, public communication), the subjective (inward, private understanding), and the physical elements. This somewhat enigmatic array of symbols implies a complete universe which can be ordered and interpreted through signs, symbols and language. The yellow and black of the banner, according to Mullican's system of color coding, represent the arts ("the world framed") and language. These signs are an attempt to explore the contruction of meaning and are excerpted from a larger order of categorization developed by Mullican.

Jean Nouvel's mixed-media installation *Ecosystem* evokes

the quick and constantly changing visual experience of cities. Nouvel condenses aspects of street scenes through an assemblage of common equipment and hardware found in any city. Street reflectors, flashing traffic lights, and construction materials are removed from their everyday context and are mined for aesthetic content instead of being ignored or taken for granted. Nouvel writes that his work re-creates "for the urban dweller fleeting aesthetic experiences," a reminder that the visual chaos we perceive daily on the streets is actually an intense visual experience. In order to understand aesthetics today, we must deal with the nature of this phenomenon and its impact on our perception.

Inspired by a visit to the Antwerp Zoo (Belgium) where the animals live in miniature re-creations of past architecture (i.e., monkeys and reptiles in a Greek ruin; rhinoceroses in a Swiss chalet), **Joel Otterson** has created a zoo and park on wheels in *The Cage (The Living Room).* This compact and mobile unit offers a whimsical perspective on nature's place in the busy, over crowded urban environment. It also alludes to the roles of zoos and museums as the preserves of both nature and culture. The elaborate skyscraper-shaped cages, built out of an unlikely combination of copper plumbing pipes and antique 18th-century Dutch tiles and other incongruous elements, houses a group of far-from-exotic white chickens. Otterson's humor plays on city-dwellers' limited experience with nature and also spoofs conventions of modern architecture in the work's shape and form.

In *Ruin,* video art pioneer **Nam June Paik** metaphorically represents TV's enormous influence on modern society. Paik arranges 45 "antique" television consoles and 24 state-of-the-art monitors into a mock city skyline. The new equipment plays video tapes that feature the New York cityscape. Paik uses the television as a symbol of modern culture's preoccupation with the new and our tendency to discard the old. Paik reminds us that along with the rapid technological development in our culture, we create new definitions for antiquity and obsolescence. The cabinets, for example, though only 30 years old, are accorded the status of antiquated relics.

In *Cymbal,* **Liz Phillips** offers an alternative to our normal, assaultive experience of sound in the city by creating a multilayered, interactive sound environment which responds to the presence of the viewer. Phillips utilizes a sophisticated system of ultrasonic sensors to locate people in the space. The sound program registers movement, stillness and the distance between people as they move through the space, generating sounds accordingly and also bouncing sound off a series of Plexiglas panels. The subtly shifting dynamic between the participants, the acoustical program and the installation's architectural framework sensitizes the viewer to ambient sound in the larger context of the city.

In *Face*, **Robert Price** has stripped open an existing wall of the building to reveal its normally concealed inner workings. The remaining surface is covered with images stenciled on aluminum panels, each referring to a particular way of looking at the "skin" of the earth from macrocosmic to microcosmic levels. The five tiers incorporate photographic studies of skin cells and radar images of hurricanes and oceanographic currents, fault lines, and a map of Manhattan. Price's sculpture plays on different meanings of the word "face," as well as the infinite variety of faces that make up the earth's surfaces and/or comprise our ways of seeing them.

In *Turf Parterre Garden*, **Martha Schwartz** has designed a skewed grid made of artificial grass and bare earth, which unrolls across the lawn beginning at the highway's edge and continuing up the building facade. The grid pattern matches the window design of Cesar Pelli's architecture. The intentional use of synthetic materials to create this unusual landscape garden raises issues of the "real" as opposed to the "artificial," alluding to 19th-century English gardens through her combination of organic and man-made elements. She also addresses the role of landscape design in the urban environment, often considered secondary to architectural design. In *Turf Parterre Garden* she creates a literal and metaphoric garden which emphasizes her focus on landscape and architecture as related design elements.

Haim Steinbach humorously re-creates a pastoral scene in the midst of an urban setting in *Adirondack Tableau*. Steinbach uses objects ordinarily found in a rural milieu, thereby simulating a setting quite distinct from and foreign to The World Financial Center. A cedar wall stands with two Adirondack benches on either side; two carved owls are set into the wall's cutout window. Sitting on the benches, the viewer looks out either onto city streets or The World Financial Center's plaza with the Hudson River and New Jersey cities beyond; by so doing, the viewer also becomes part of this artificial tableau, engaged in this mock encounter with nature. Steinbach states that he is "interested in devising a model which, like a gameboard, defines a ground for play." *Adirondack Tableau* represents an ironic commentary on the city-dweller's romantic notion or memory of rustic settings.

Mierle Laderman Ukeles extols the unsung, ordinary workers who make the city function in her sculpture, *Ceremonial Arch Honoring Service Workers in the New Service Economy*.

Ukeles uses the triumphal arch, which traditionally commemorates military achievements, as a tribute to the thousands of people who labor anonymously in the urban infrastructure. The steel arch is composed of service-specific materials used to represent various trades as well as thousands of gloves, including those of workers from twelve municipal, state and federal agencies and public utilities, many of which are signed by the workers who wore them. Similarly there are references to the lands from which people have emigrated for the freedom to work and live in New York. Ukeles' work, like many others in the exhibition, involves the viewer in a reexamination of the people who make up the fabric of the city.

In *14 Arborvitae*, **Jacques Vieille** has built an artificial grove of trees using a thin wood lathe and living plants. The gently curving structures suggest both a protection of the living plants as well as a cage for their containment and inhibition. Vieille speaks to the essential dichotomy between the natural and unnatural predicaments imposed by processes of advancing civilization.

Both the isolation and the compression that characterize living in the city are evoked in **Richard Wentworth's** *Neighbour, Neighbour*. Two empty steel houses are bolted together and suspended from the ceiling. They share a common wall which is penetrated by a series of holes plugged by corks. The two linked yet separate houses suggest a relationship in which people share housing and office space, but are nevertheless separated and isolated from each other by individual choices and circumstances as well as by architecture itself. Wentworth also notes, "It is typical of cities that opposites rub against each other and that the gap between differences is compressed to a minimum."

Stephen Willats examines the relationship between people, buildings and objects in his *Signs and Messages from Corporate America*. The artist documented office environments within The World Financial Center: people, equipment, personal effects, signage and sounds. With his enlarged and irregularly framed photographs, Willats offers the viewer a new look at the workplace, subtly manipulating our perspective in the manner of advertising. The impact of large, glossy photos suggests the general and symbolic; the quirky framing adds an element of the individualistic to the slick mass-media format. The subject matter combines items of ubiquitous commercial presence with idiosyncratic, highly personal objects, giving insights into how people try to assert their individuality despite identical work stations and conformity-inducing rules.

ELIZABETH ZESCHIN SEVEN

118

PHOTOGRAPHS

Richard Martin is the Executive Director of the Shirley Goodman Resource Center of the Fashion Institute of Technology and is the author of *Fashion and Surrealism* and *Jocks and Nerds*. He lives in New York City.

Herbert Muschamp is the architectural critic for *Artforum* and *The New Republic* and directs the Graduate Program in Criticism at Parsons School of Design. He lives in New York City.

CONTRIBUTORS

Writers

Douglas Blau is an art critic living in New York City.

Rosetta Brooks is a writer living in New York City and is the editor of *ZG Magazine* as well as a regular contributor to *Artforum*, *Flash Art*, *Art News*, and *C.*

Bruce W. Ferguson is a curator and critic living in New York City.

Adam Gopnik is an editor and staff writer at *The New Yorker*. He lives in Soho.

Elizabeth Hardwick is a critic and novelist who lives in New York City. Her most recent works include *Sleepless Nights*, a novel, and *Bartleby in Manhattan*, a series of essays.

Dave Hickey is a free-lance writer who lives in San Diego, California.

Sanford Kwinter is an editor of *Zone* and lives and teaches in New York City.

Dr. Mark J. Plotkin is the Director of Plant Conservation at the World Wildlife Fund and also serves on the staff of The Botanical Museum of Harvard University. He lives in Washington, D.C.

Nancy Princenthal is a free-lance critic whose writing has appeared in *Art in America*, *The Village Voice*, *Art News*, *Artforum*, *The Print Collector's Newsletter* and other publications. She lives in New York City.

Mark Richard is the author of a collection of short stories, *The Ice at the Bottom of the World*, published by Alfred A. Knopf. His work has appeared in *Esquire*, *Shenandoah*, *The Quarterly*, *Antaeus*, *Grand Street* and *Equator* magazines. He lives in New York City.

PHOTOGRAPHERS

Jon Abbott is an artist who free-lances as a photographer. He lives in New York City. *Pages 57-73, 76-79, 81-83, 86-91, 94-99, 102-111.*

David McGlynn is a photographer living and working in New York City. His work has been extensively exhibited, and published in many periodicals, including *Life*, *Interview*, *Metropolitan Home* and *Condé Nast Traveler*. *Pages 30-33.*

Elizabeth Zeschin is a photographer who specializes in travel, interiors and gardens. Her work has appeared in *Vogue*, *HG* and *Connoisseur*, among others. She lives in New York City. *Pages 188, 122/123.*

Other Photo Credits:

Peter Aaron/ESTO, *page 13.*

Sally Boon, *pages 78/79.*

T. Charles Erickson, *page 74.*

Dan Graham, *pages 66/67.*

Robin Holland, *pages 10-12, 16/17, 80, 84/85, 92/93, 101.*

Wolfgang Hoyt, *pages 56, 117.*

Dona Ann McAdams, *pages 10, 13, 16.*

Rita Nanini, *pages 10, 14-17.*

Robert Walker, *page 100.*

The photos on the front and back covers and page 36 are courtesy of **Con Edison,** and depict "The Making of the City of Light," New York World's Fair, 1938/39.

BIOGRAPHIES

Vito Acconci (b. 1940), American
Garden with Fountain, 1988

Special Thanks: Gary Higgonson, Brownie Johnson, David Licht, Michael Morris, Jim Schmidt, Luis Vera, Robert Wesseldyke

Holy Cross College, Worcester, MA (B.A., 1962)
University of Iowa, Iowa City (M.F.A., 1964)

Resides in Brooklyn, NY

Selected Solo Exhibitions:

1985 The Brooklyn Museum, New York

Wadsworth Atheneum, Hartford, CT

1987 La Jolla Museum of Contemporary Art, CA

Neuberger Museum, Purchase, NY

Laumeier Sculpture Park, St. Louis, MO

Aspen Art Museum, CO

1988 The Museum of Modern Art, New York

Selected Group Exhibitions:

1985 Artpark, Lewiston, NY

"Biennale des Freidens," Kunsthaus und Kunstverein, Hamburg, Germany

"Making Shelter," Graduate School of Architecture and Design, Harvard University, Cambridge, MA

"Vème Biennale Internationale de Sculpture en Plein Air," Skironio Museum Polychronopoulos, Athens, Greece

1986 "Single Shots: A Video History of Personal Expression," Institute of Contemporary Art, Boston, MA

1987 "Perverted by Language," Hillwood Art Gallery, C.W. Post Campus, Long Island University, Greenvale, NY

Dennis Adams/Andrea Blum
Landfill: Bus Station, 1988

Dennis Adams (b. 1948), American

Drake University, Des Moines (B.F.A., 1969)
Tyler School of Art, Philadelphia (M.F.A., 1971)

Resides in New York

Selected Public Projects:

1985 "Creative Time: Art on the Beach," New York: a collaboration with Nicholas Goldsmith, FTL Associates and Ann Magnuson: *A Podium for Dissent*

1986 "Bus Shelter II," 14th Street and 3rd Avenue, Public Art Fund, New York

1987 "Building Against Image," Alternative Museum, New York

City University Graduate Center Mall, New York: *Out of Service*

"Skulptur Projekte Münster," Westfalisches Landesmuseum, Münster, West Germany: *Bus Shelter IV*

1988 "Bus Shelter VIII," Cold City Gallery, Toronto, Canada

"Reworking," Halle Sud, Geneva, Switzerland

"Bezugspunkte 38/88," Steirischer Herbst, Graz, Austria: *Fallen Angels*

"Public Commands/Other Voices," The New Music America Festival, Miami, FL

Andrea Blum (b. 1950), American

Boston Museum School of Fine Arts/Tufts University, MA (B.F.A., 1973)
School of the Art Institute of Chicago, IL (M.F.A., 1976)

Selected Public Projects:

1984 "Livonia," Art in Public Places Commission, Livonia, MI (completed 1988)

1985 "Street Link," Sunrise Park, Dayton, OH (completed 1988)

1987 Carlsbad Cultural Arts Commission for City of Carlsbad, CA

"107th Street Pier Renovation," collaboration with Giorgio Cavaglieri and Joseph Sultan, architects, New York

"Newstand Project," collaboration with Ken Kaplan and Ted Kruger, architects; Public Art Fund, New York

"Rotational Shift," Wisconsin State Arts Commission, Computer Science Building Plaza, University of Wisconsin, Madison, WI

Adams/Blum Collaborative Project:

1988 "Linear Park," a collaboration with Martha Schwartz and Peter Walker, C.C.D.C. and Marina Redevelopment Corporation, San Diego, CA

Kim Adams (b. 1951), Canadian
Chameleon Unit, 1988

Special Thanks: The Canada Council, Mike Coughlin, Reid Diamond, The Double Door in Anten Mills, Barbara Fischer, Sarah Fraser, Beverly Gordon, Laurie McFarlane, Peter McFarlane, The Ontario Arts Council, Stephen Parkinson, David Winter

Resides in Toronto, Canada

Selected Solo Exhibitions:

1984 Contemporary Arts Forum, Santa Barbara, CA

1987 Ydessa Gallery, Toronto, Canada

1988 Galerie Christiane Chassay, Montreal, Canada

Selected Group Exhibitions:

1986 "The Interpretation of Architecture," organized by YYZ, Toronto, The Surrey Art Gallery, Canada

1987 "São Paulo Bienale," Brazil

1988 "On Track," Calgary Winter Olympics, Canada

Three Rivers Arts Festival, Pittsburgh, PA

Judith Barry (b. 1949), American
Adam's Wish, 1988

Special Thanks: Acadia Scenic, Jersey City, NJ; Caesar Video Graphics, New York

University of Florida, Gainesville (B.S., 1972)
New York Institute of Technology (M.A., 1986)

Resides in New York

Selected Solo Exhibitions:

1986 "Projects 2," The Museum of Modern Art, New York: *Echo*

1987 COCA Natural Foods Pavilion, Seattle, WA

1988 Douglas Hyde Gallery, Dublin, Ireland: *Echo/In the shadow of the city . . . vampry*

Selected Group Exhibitions:

1986 "Damaged Goods," The New Museum of Contemporary Art, New York

1987 "Biennial," Whitney Museum of American Art, New York; *First and Third*

1988 "Loie Fuller: Dance of Colors," Performance/Lighting Design with Brygida Ochaim; Biennale de Danse, Lyon and Nouvelles Scenes, Dijon, France

"Venice Biennale," Italy: *Aperto*

"Expanded Forms," Whitney Museum of American Art at Equitable Center, New York

Alan Belcher (b. 1957), Canadian
Office Complex '88, 1988

Resides in Toronto, Canada

Selected Solo Exhibitions:

1985 "Made in New York," Cable Gallery, New York

1987 "Travelling Exhibition," Margo Leavin Gallery, Los Angeles, CA

1988 Daniel Buchholtz Gallery, Cologne, Germany

Josh Baer Gallery, New York

Selected Group Exhibitions:

1982 "Summer Exhibition," Nature Morte, New York

1985 "Infotainment," Texas Gallery, Houston; Rhona Hoffman Gallery, Chicago, IL; Vanguard Gallery, Philadelphia, PA; Aspen Art Museum, CO

"Split/Vision," Artists Space, New York

"Transitional Objects," Galerie Philippe Nelson, Lyon, France

1986 "Public Art," Nexus Contemporary Art Center, Atlanta, GA

"As Found," Institute of Contemporary Art, Boston, MA

1987 "Les Courtiers du Desire," Centre Georges Pompidou, Paris, France

Metro Pictures, New York

1988 "Reprises De Vues," Halle Sud, Geneva, Switzerland

"Presi Per Incantamento," Padiglione d'Art Contemporanea, Milan, Italy

"Publics Art," Cold City Gallery, Toronto, Canada

Dan Graham (b. 1942), American
Triangular Structure with Two-Way Mirror Sliding Door, 1988

Special Thanks: Joe Jaroff, Mison Concepts; Ken Saylor

Resides in New York

Selected Solo Exhibitions:

1985 Art Gallery of Western Australia, Perth

1986 Kijkhuis, The Hague, Holland

1987 ARC, Musée d'Art Moderne del la Ville de Paris, France

Centro de Arte Reina Sofia, Madrid, Spain

Selected Group Exhibitions:

1985 "The Art of Memory: The Loss of History," The New Museum of Contemporary Art, New York

"New Video Acquisitions," The Museum of Modern Art, New York

1986 "Chambres d'Amis," Ghent, Belgium

1987 "1967: At the Crossroads," Institute of Contemporary Art, University of Pennsylvania, Philadelphia

"Biennial," Whitney Museum of American Art, New York

"Skulptur Projekte Münster," Westfalisches Landesmuseum, Münster, Germany

Susan Hiller (b. 1942), American
Monument, 1981-1988

Special Thanks: David Coxhead, Tim Guest

Resides in London, England

Selected Solo Exhibitions:

1984-85 Third Eye Center, Glasgow, Scotland; Orchard Gallery, Londonderry, United Kingdom; Gimpel Fils, London, England

1986 Institute of Contemporary Art, London, England

1988 California State University Gallery, Long Beach, CA

Interim Art, London, England

Pat Hearn Gallery, New York

Selected Group Exhibitions:

1985 "The British Show," British Arts Council: Art Gallery of Western Australia, Perth; Art Gallery of New South Wales, Sydney; Queensland Art Gallery, Brisbane; Royal Exhibition Building, Melbourne, Australia

1986 "Staging The Self," National Portrait Gallery, London, England

"Force of Circumstance," P.P.O.W. Gallery, New York

1987 "Towards a Bigger Picture," Victoria & Albert Museum, London, England

"Current Affairs," Museum of Modern Art, Oxford, England; National Gallery, Prague, Czechoslovakia; Zacheta, Warsaw, Poland; Muscarnot, Budapest, Hungary

1988 "British Art: The Literate Link," Asher/Faure Gallery, Los Angeles, CA

Hodgetts + Fung
Near Things, 1988

Special Thanks: Frank Clementi

Craig Hodgetts (b. 1937), American

Yale University, New Haven, CT (M.Arch., 1967)

Resides in Santa Monica, CA

Hsing-Ming Fung (b. 1953), American

California State College, Dominguez Hills (B.A., 1977)
University of California, Los Angeles (M.Arch., 1980)

Resides in Santa Monica, CA

Selected Collaborative Projects:

1987 "Case Study Exhibition," Museum of Contemporary Art, Los Angeles, CA

1988 C.I.S. Production Facilities, Los Angeles, CA

"UCLA Gateway," Los Angeles, CA

Selected Collaborative Exhibitions:

1984 "84/84 Olympic Architects," Museum of Science and Industry, Los Angeles, CA

1987 "Buenos Aires Architecture Biennial," Argentina

"The Emerging Generation in U.S.A.," G.A. Gallery, Tokyo, Japan

1988 "The Experimental Tradition," National Academy of Design, New York

"L.A. Architecture: 12 + 12—An Overview," Pacific Design Center, Los Angeles, CA

Henry Jesionka (b. 1957), Canadian
Nullstadt, 1988

Special Thanks: Air Canada; Consulate General of Canada, New York; Fresnel Products, Rochester, NY; Juan Geuer, Hall Train Animations, Toronto, Canada; Edward Jesionka, Level Seven Research, Toronto, Canada

Ryerson Polytechnical Institute, Toronto (B.A.A., 1982)
State University of New York, Buffalo, Center for Media Study (M.A., 1985)

Resides in Vancouver, Canada

Selected Installations:

1985 Spaulding Hall, Buffalo, NY: *Artificial Insemination*

1987 "Re-Animators," Hallwalls, Buffalo, NY: *Intravenous Divinities*

1988 "Social Studies," Artists Space, New York: *White House*

Selected Screenings:

1985 "Festival of Festivals," Toronto Canada: *Resurrected Fields*

1986 "Ars Electronica," Linz, Austria: *Songs of Pluriverse*

Kristin Jones and Andrew Ginzel
Geotaxis, 1988

Special Thanks: Bryan Gill, Jerry Lerner, Pedro Norde, David Nyzio, Greg Sale, Gary Simmons

Kristin Jones (b. 1956), American

Rhode Island School of Design, Providence (B.F.A., 1979)
Yale University, New Haven, CT (M.F.A., 1983)

Resides in New York

Andrew Ginzel (b. 1954), American

Bennington College, VT (1972-1974)
State University of New York (1978-1981)

Resides in New York

Selected Collaborative Installations:

1986 Virginia Museum of Fine Arts, Richmond: *Ephemeris*

The New Museum of Contemporary Art, New York: *Triptych*

1987 City Hall Park, Public Art Fund, New York: *Pananemone*

1988 Wadsworth Atheneum, Matrix 99, Hartford, CT: *Seraphim* and *Analemma*

M.I.T. Visual Arts Center, Cambridge, MA: *Charybdis*

Annina Nosei Gallery, New York: *Metathesis*

Michael Kalil (b. 1944), American
Elysian Field III A, 1988

Special Thanks: Peter Barna, Dale Goncher, Ed Lally

Resides in New York

Selected Projects:

1971 "The Bilgore Apartment Competition," New York: *Elysian Field I*

1983 "Electronic Pavilion (Home Office)" for Armstrong World Industries, Lancaster, PA

1983 "Space Station Habitation," for NASA, Washington, DC (ongoing)

Selected Group Exhibitions:

1985 "High Styles," Whitney Museum of American Art, New York

1986 "From Here to Eternity," Artists Space, New York

1988 "Civilized Life," Art Awareness, Lexington, NY: *Sky Garden*

Tadashi Kawamata (b. 1953), Japanese
Favela in Battery Park City: Inside/Outside, 1988

Special Thanks: Mika Koike, Sang Joo, On The Table, Tokyo Storefront for Art and Architecture

Resides in Tokyo, Japan

Selected Projects:

1985 "Limelight," New York

"P.S. 1 Project," New York

1987 "La Maison des Squatters," Grenoble, France

"Documenta 8," Kassel, West Germany: *Destroyed Church*

"São Paulo Bienale," Brazil: *Project Nove de Julho Cacapava*

1988 "Rooftop Project," The Institute for Art and Urban Resources, P.S. 1, New York

"Roosevelt Island Project," James Renwick Building, New York

Jon Kessler (b. 1957), American
Exodus, 1988

Special Thanks: Jordan Plitteris

State University of New York, Purchase
(B.F.A., 1980)
Whitney Museum Independent Study,
Studio Program, New York (1981)

Resides in Brooklyn, NY

Selected Solo Exhibitions:

1983 Artists Space, New York

1986 Museum of Contemporary Art,
Chicago, IL; Cincinnati Art Center, OH;
Contemporary Arts Museum, Houston,
TX

1987 Luhring, Augustine & Hodes
Gallery, New York

1988 Galerie Max Hetzler, Cologne,
Germany

Selected Group Exhibitions:

1984 "International Survey of Recent
Painting and Sculpture," The Museum of
Modern Art, New York

1985 "Biennial," Whitney Museum of
American Art, New York

"São Paulo Bienale," Brazil

1986 "End Game: Reference and
Simulation," Institute of Contemporary
Art, Boston, MA

"Byron-Kessler," Galerie Barbara Farber,
Amsterdam, Holland

"New Trends/New Technique: Advances
in World Sculpture," Contemporary
Sculpture Center, Tokyo; Contemporary
Sculpture Center, Osaka, Japan

"Forg, Gober, Hutte, Kessler, Kiecol,
Koons, Meuser, Zobernig," Galerie Max
Hetzler, Cologne, Germany

1987 "Investigations," Institute of
Contemporary Art, University of Pennsylvania, Philadelphia

1988 "St. Clair Cemin, Joel Fisher, Jon
Kessler, Joel Otterson," Massimo Audiello
Gallery, New York

"Graz 1988," Staatsmuseum, Graz, Austria

Kunst Brothers (b. 1987)
Volta/Votive, 1988

Special Thanks: Michael Dunn, Editel
New York, Pat Ferris, Joe Klotz, Michael
Pyles

Kunst Brothers is a *nom de guerre* for the
collaborative work of painter/sculptor
Alison Saar and computer/video artist
Tom Leeser.

Alison Saar (b. 1956), American

Scripps College, Claremont, CA (B.A.,
1978)
Otis Art Institute, Los Angeles, CA
(M.F.A., 1981)

Selected Solo Exhibitions:

1986 Monique Knowlton Gallery, New
York

Washington Project for the Arts, Washington, DC

1988 Jan Baum Gallery, Los Angeles, CA

Selected Group Exhibitions:

1984 "American Women Artists," Sidney
Janis Gallery, New York

1985 "Since the Harlem Renaissance,"
Bucknell University, Lewisberg, PA

1987 "Recent Acquisitions," Metropolitan
Museum of Art, New York

Tom Leeser (b. 1956), American

San Francisco Art Institute, CA (B.F.A.,
1976; M.F.A., 1978)

Selected Solo Exhibitions:

1983 Hampshire College, Amherst, MA

Millenium, New York

Selected Group Exhibitions:

1984 "Festival for New Experimental
Cinema," Chicago Art Institute, IL

1985 "Made for TV Festival," Institute of
Contemporary Art, Boston, MA

1987 "The Second Emerging Expression
Biennial: The Artist and The Computer,"
Bronx Museum of the Arts, NY

Justen Ladda (b. 1953), German
Romeo and Juliet, 1988

Special Thanks: Marlene Marta

Resides in New York

Selected Solo Exhibitions:

1986 "Projects," The Museum of Modern
Art, New York

1987 The Israel Museum, Jerusalem:
1+1=2

1988 San Diego State University Art
Gallery, CA and Galerie Lelong, New
York: *Simulation Meltdown*

Selected Group Exhibitions:

1984 "Arte Di Frontiera," Galleria
Communale d'Arte Moderna, Bologna,
Italy

"A Different Climate," Kunstalle,
Düsseldorf, Germany

1986 "Damaged Goods," The New
Museum of Contemporary Art, New York

"Reality Remade," Kent Fine Art, New
York

Morphosis
Room Compressed, 1988

Special Thanks: Mison Concepts

Thom Mayne (b. 1944), American

University of Southern California, Los
Angeles (B.Arch., 1968)
Harvard University, Cambridge, MA
(M.Arch., 1978)

Resides in Santa Monica, CA

Michael Rotundi (b. 1949), American

Southern California Institute of Architecture, Santa Monica (Diploma, 1973)

Resides in Silverlake, CA

Selected Morphosis Collaborative Projects:

1982 Chrisman-Bergren Residence,
Venice, CA (completed 1984)

1986 Kate Mantilini Restaurant, Los
Angeles, CA

1988 Cedar-Sinai Comprehensive Cancer
Center, Los Angeles, CA

6th Street Residence, Venice, CA

Selected Collaborative Exhibitions:

1982 "The California Condition," La
Jolla Museum of Contemporary Art, CA

1983 "California Counterpoint,"
National Academy of Design, New York

1985 "California Architecture —
Morphosis/Eric Owen Moss," G.A.
Gallery, Tokyo, Japan

1987 "The Emerging Generation in
U.S.A.," G.A. Gallery, Tokyo, Japan

Can a city maintain a memory

Matt Mullican (b. 1951), American
Untitled, 1988

Special Thanks: Ace Banner, Robert Fosdick, Mison Concepts

California Institute of the Arts, Valencia (B.F.A., 1974)

Resides in New York

Selected Solo Exhibitions:

1987 Dallas Museum of Art, TX; "Concentration 15"

Moore College of Art, Philadelphia, PA; "Banners, Monuments and the City"

1988 Bath International Festival, England

Winnipeg Art Gallery, Canada; Manufrance, Saint Etienne; F.R.A.C., Rhone-Alps, France; The Brooklyn Museum, NY; San Diego State University, CA

Selected Group Exhibitions:

1982 "Documenta 7," Kassel, Germany

1986 "Maelstrom," Palais des Beaux Arts, Brussels, Belgium

"Art and Its Double," Fundación Caja de Pensiones, Madrid, Spain

"The Spiritual in Art: Abstract Painting 1890-1985," Los Angeles County Museum of Art, CA; Museum of Contemporary Art, Chicago, IL

"Individuals: A Selected History of California Artists, 1945-1985," Museum of Contemporary Art, Los Angeles, CA

1987 "Avant Garde in the 80s," Los Angeles County Museum of Art, CA

"L'Epoque, La Mode, La Morale, La Passion," Centre Georges Pompidou, Paris, France

"CalArts: Skeptical Belief(s)," The Renaissance Society of the University of Chicago, IL; The Newport Harbor Art Museum, CA

"Skulptur Projekte Münster," Westfalisches Landesmuseum, Münster, Germany

1988 "Sculptures de Chambres," Centre D'Art Contemporain, Geneva, Switzerland

Jean Nouvel (b. 1945), French
Ecosystem, 1988

Special Thanks: Perl Electronics, Alain Trincal

École Nationale Superieure des Beaux-Arts, Paris (D.P.L.G., 1971)

Resides in Paris, France

Selected Current Projects:

1985 C.N.R.S. Documentation Center, Nancy, France

1986 Opera House, Lyon, France

1988 Health and Beauty Center, Perrier Group, Vichy, France

Selected Completed Projects:

1980 Belfort Theatre, France with Gilbert Lézénès and Dominique Lyon, constructed 1982-1984

1981 The Institute of the Arab World, Paris, France with Pierre Soria, Gilbert Lézénès and Architecture Studio, constructed 1982-1987

1982 Social Housing, 48 apartments, Saint-Ouen, France with Pierre Soria and Gilbert Lézénès, constructed 1985-1987

1985 Nemausus 1, 114 apartments, Nîmes, France with Jean-Marc Ibos, constructed 1986-1987

Joel Otterson (b. 1959), American
The Cage (The Living Room), 1988

Special Thanks: Randy Otterson, Kees Van Der Ploeg

Parsons School of Design, New York (B.F.A., 1982)

Resides in New York

Selected Solo Exhibitions:

1987 Nature Morte, New York

"Projects," The Museum of Modern Art, New York

Selected Group Exhibitions:

1985 "Smart Art," Carpenter Center for the Visual Arts, Harvard University, Cambridge, MA

"Infotainment," Texas Gallery, Houston; Rhona Hoffman Gallery, Chicago, IL; Vanguard Gallery, Philadelphia, PA; The Aspen Art Museum, CO

"Affiliations: Recent Sculpture and Its Antecedents," Whitney Museum of American Art, Stamford, CT

1986 "Endgame: Reference and Simulation," Institute of Contemporary Art, Boston, MA

1987 "Sarah Charlesworth/Joel Otterson," Margo Leavin Gallery, Los Angeles, CA

"The New Poverty," John Gibson Gallery, New York

1988 Massimo Audiello Gallery, New York

Jay Gorney Modern Art, New York

Sidney Janis Gallery, New York

Laurie Rubin Gallery, New York

"Art at The End of The Social," Rooseum Museum, Stockholm, Sweden

Nam June Paik (b. 1932), American
Ruin, 1988

Special Thanks: Paul Garrin, Mark Patsfall

University of Tokyo (B.A., 1956)

Resides in New York

Selected Solo Exhibitions:

1982 Whitney Museum of American Art, New York; Museum of Contemporary Art, Chicago, IL

1986 "Nam June Paik: Sculpture, Painting and Laser Photography," Holly Solomon Gallery, New York

1988 "Nam June Paik: Family of Robot," The Hayward Gallery, South Bank Center, London, England

Selected Group Exhibitions:

1984 "XLI Esposizione Internazionale la Biennale di Venezia," Venice, Italy

1985 "São Paulo Bienale," Brazil

1987 "Documenta 8," Kassel, Germany

"L'Epoque, La Mode, La Morale, La Passion," Centre Georges Pompidou, Paris, France

"Biennial," Whitney Museum of American Art, New York

1988 "Positions in Art Today," The National Gallery, Berlin, Germany

of the land on which it is built?

Liz Phillips (b. 1951), American
Cymbal, 1988

Special Thanks: Analogue Digital Systems, Philip Edelstein, Kan Kanzaki, George Lewis, National Endowment for the Arts through Lower Manhattan Cultural Council Foundation, New York State Council on the Arts through Parabola Arts Foundation, Polaroid Corporation, San Diego State University Arts Council, Serge Tcherepnin

Bennington College, VT (B.A., 1973)

Resides in New York

Selected Solo Exhibitions:

1981 Creative Time, Bronx Frontier Development Ranch, New York: *Windspun*

1982 Walker Art Center, Minneapolis, MN: *Sound Syzygy*

1983 Wadsworth Atheneum, Hartford, CT: *Sunspots*

1984 Walker Art Center, University of Minnesota, and KUOM, Minneapolis: *Zephyr*

1985 San Diego State University Art Gallery, CA: *Cymbal*

Jacob's Pillow, Lee, MA: *Sound Syzygy*

1988 Whitney Museum of American Art, New York: *Graphic Ground*

Selected Group Exhibitions:

1981 "New Music America '81," San Francisco Museum of Modern Art, CA: *Sunspots*

1984 "Think Pockets," IBM, Tokyo, Japan: *Sunspots*

1985 "Biennial," Whitney Museum of American Art, New York: *Whitney Windspun*

1986 "Engaging Objects," The Clocktower, New York: *Sound Syzygy*

1987 "Spoleto USA," Charleston, SC: *Cymbal*

"Ars Electronica," Linz, Austria: *Windspun*

Robert Price (b. 1950), American
Face, 1988

Special Thanks: Mark Simpson

University of Washington, Seattle (B.F.A., 1975)
Columbia University, New York (M.F.A., 1979)

Resides in Brooklyn, NY

Selected Solo Exhibitions:

1987 Cable Gallery, New York

Selected Group Exhibitions:

1984 "Modern/Post Modern Sculpture," Kenkeleba Gallery, New York

1988 "NYC #1 Sculpture," Galerie Westersingel 8, Rotterdam, Holland

"A Drawing Show," Cable Gallery, New York

Martha Schwartz (b. 1950), American
Turf Parterre Garden, 1988

Special Thanks: Robert Fosdick and crew, Ken Smith

University of Michigan, Ann Arbor (B.F.A., 1973; M.F.A., 1977)
Harvard University Graduate School of Design, Landscape Architecture Program, Boston (1976-77)

Resides in San Francisco, CA, and New York

Selected Projects:

1980 The Bagel Garden, Boston, MA

Necco/Tire Garden, M.I.T., Cambridge, MA

1983 King County Correctional Facilities, Seattle, WA: *Entrance Garden*

1986 The Whitehead Institute Rooftop, Cambridge, MA

1988 Office for the Arts at Harvard and Radcliffe, Cambridge, MA: *Limed Parterre with Sky-writer*

Haim Steinbach (b. 1944), American
Adironack Tableau, 1988

Special Thanks: Matthew Droege, Ken Heitz, Alan Irikura, Henry Tomkalsky, David Winter

Pratt Institute, Brooklyn, NY (B.F.A., 1968)
Yale University, New Haven, CT (M.F.A., 1973)

Resides in Brooklyn, NY

Selected Solo Exhibitions:

1987 Sonnabend Gallery, New York

1988 Jay Gorney Modern Art, New York

"CAPC," Musée d'Art Contemporain, Bordeaux, France: *Recent Work*

Selected Group Exhibitions:

1985 "Infotainment," Texas Gallery, Houston; Rhona Hoffman Gallery, Chicago, IL; Vanguard Gallery, Philadelphia, PA; Aspen Art Museum, CO

1986 "Art and Its Double," Fundación Caja de Pensiones, Madrid, Spain

1987 "Les Courtiers Du Desir," Centre Georges Pompidou, Paris, France

"Avant Garde In The Eighties," Los Angeles County Museum of Art, CA

1988 "Cultural Geometry," Deste Foundation for Contemporary Art, Athens, Greece

"New York In View," Kunstverein München, Munich, Germany

Mierle Laderman Ukeles (b. 1939), American
Ceremonial Arch Honoring Service Workers in the New Service Economy, 1988

Special Thanks: New York City Department of Cultural Affairs, New York City Department of Environmental Protection, New York City Fire Department, New York City Department of Parks and Recreation, New York City Police Department, New York City Department of Sanitation, New York City Department of Transportation, Metropolitan Transportation Authority, U.S. Post Office, Consolidated Edison, New York Telephone, Olympia & York and Daniel Carello, Rachel Clark, Leszek Gesien, Elka Gould, Samuel Harris, Jane Hill, Pat Hough, Richard Humann, David Hurd, Andrew Kettler, Cynthia Kuebel, Maria Levitsky, Julie Overskei, Sarah Rodgers, J. David Shaw, Debby Spinelli and Yoan Yu

Barnard College, New York (B.A., 1961)
New York University (M.A., 1974)

Resides in New York

Selected Projects:

1983 "Sanitations Celebrations, NYC"

1983-90 "Flow City," 59th Street Marine Transfer Station on the Hudson River, NYC Department of Sanitation, New York

1987 "Out of the Studio: Art with Community," The Institute for Art and Urban Resources, P.S. 1, Long Island City, NY: *Re-entry*

1988 "Light Up Philadelphia," Fairmont Park Art Association, Philadelphia, PA

Selected Group Exhibitions:

1985 "After Tilted Arc," Storefront for Art and Architecture, New York

1988 "Selected Entries from the Visions for Penn's Fifth Square: Philadelphia City Hall Centennial Design Competition," City Hall and Marian Locks Gallery, Philadelphia, PA

Jacques Vieille (b. 1948), French
14 Arborvitae, 1986-1988

Resides in Clessé (Saone-et-Loire), France

Selected Solo Exhibitions:

1984 Centre Georges Pompidou, Paris, France

1985 Joan Miró Foundation, Espace 10, Barcelona, Spain

1986 Art Contemporain, Ecole des Beaux-Arts, Mâcon, France

1987 La Criée, Halle d'Art Contemporain, Rennes, France

Musée Cantonal des Beaux-Arts, Sion (Haute-Savoie), France

Selected Group Exhibitions:

1987 "Documenta 8," Kassel, Germany

Richard Wentworth (b. 1947), English
Neighbour, Neighbour, 1988

Hornsey College of Art, London (1965)
Royal College of Art, London (1966-1970)

Resides in London, England

Selected Solo Exhibitions:

1986 Lisson Gallery, London, England

1987 Riverside Studios, London, England

1988 Wolff Gallery, New York

Sala Parpallo, Valencia, Spain

Selected Group Exhibitions:

1985 "The British Show," British Arts Council: Art Gallery of Western Australia, Perth; Art Gallery of New South Wales, Sydney; Queensland Art Gallery, Brisbane; Royal Exhibition Building, Melbourne, Australia

1986 "Sculpture: Nine Artists from Britain," Louisiana Museum, Humelbaek, Denmark

1987 "Object Lessons," The Banff Centre, Walter Phillips Gallery, Canada

1988 "British Sculpture 1968-86," Tate of the North, Liverpool, England

Stephen Willats (b. 1943), English
Signs and Messages from Corporate America, 1988

Special Thanks: Joel Livet, Merrill Lynch & Co., Inc.

Ealing School of Art, London (1962-63)

Resides in London, England

Selected Solo Exhibitions:

1986 "Concepts and Models," Institute of Contemporary Art, London, England

1987 "Contemporary Living," Museum van Hedendaagse Kunst, Ghent, Belgium

1988 "Code Breakers," Torch Gallery, Amsterdam, Holland

Selected Group Exhibitions:

1984 "Sculptural Alternatives: Aspects of Photography and Sculpture in Britain, 1965-1982," Tate Gallery, London, England

1985 "The British Art Show," National Art Gallery, New Zealand

"The British Show," British Arts Council; Art Gallery of Western Australia, Perth; Art Gallery of New South Wales, Sydney; Queensland Art Gallery, Brisbane; Royal Exhibition Building, Melbourne, Australia

1986 "The Art of Peace Biennale," Kunstverein, Hamburg, Germany

1987 "Art and Craft Made and Designed in the Twentieth Century," Laing Art Gallery, Newcastle Upon Tyne, England

1988 "Triennale di Milano," Milan, Italy

MICA-TV
The New Urban Landscape, 1988

Distribution: American Federation of Art; Electronic Arts Intermix; The Kitchen; Video Data Bank, Art Institute of Chicago

Special Thanks: Bill Obrecht, Caesar Video Graphics, New York; Electric Film, New York

Carole Ann Klonarides and Michael Owen (MICA-TV) have been collaborating since 1980. Carole Ann Klonarides is an artist and independent curator and Michael Owen is an independent producer of music, commercial and industrial videos.

Carole Ann Klonarides (b. 1951), American

Virginia Commonwealth University, Richmond (B.F.A., 1973)
Whitney Museum Independent Study, Studio Program, New York (1972-73)

Resides in Brooklyn, NY

Michael Owen (b. 1951), American

The University of Essex, Colchester, England (B.A.)

Resides in New York

Selected MICA-TV Collaborative Broadcasts:

1988 "Avance Sur Image," produced by ExNihilio for Canal Plus, Paris, France

"Ghosts in the Machine," produced by John Wyver for Channel Four, England

Selected Screenings:

1984 "Video: Heroes/Anti-Heroes," Contemporary Arts Museum, Houston, TX

1985 "TV: Through the Looking Glass," The Media Alliance and New York State Museum, Albany

1986 American Museum of the Moving Image, New York

"Films on Art," Museum Boymans-Van Beuningen, Rotterdam, Holland

1987 "Video and Language," Los Angeles Contemporary Exhibitions, CA

"Video in Context," Electronic Arts Intermix and New York University Tisch School of the Arts, New York

"Digital Visions: Computers and Art," Everson Museum of Art, Syracuse, NY and IBM Gallery, New York

1988 "Cascade/Vertical Landscapes," Tom Cugliani Gallery, New York

"Collaborations," International Center of Photography, New York

"Meet The Makers," Donnell Media Center, New York Public Library, NY: *The New Urban Landscape*